Composting
inside & out

Stephanie Davies, The Urban Worm Girl

BETTERWAY HOME
CINCINNATI, OHIO
WWW.BETTERWAYBOOKS.COM

Other fine Betterway Home Books are available from your local bookstore or online or direct from the publisher. Visit our website, www.betterwaybooks.com.

15   14   13   12   11   5   4   3   2   1

Distributed in Canada by Fraser Direct
100 Armstrong Avenue, Georgetown, Ontario, Canada L7G 5S4, Tel: (905) 877-4411

Distributed in the U.K. and Europe by F+W Media International
Brunel House, Newton Abbot, Devon, TQ12 4PU, England, Tel: (+44) 1626 323200,
Fax: (+44) 1626 323319, E-mail: postmaster@davidandcharles.co.uk

Distributed in Australia by Capricorn Link
P.O. Box 704, S. Windsor NSW, 2756 Australia, Tel: (02) 4577-3555

Library of Congress Cataloging in Publication Data
Davies, Stephanie (Stephanie Linn), 1969-
   Composting inside and out : to fit your space & lifestyle / by Stephanie Davies. -- 1st ed.
      p. cm.
   ISBN 978-1-4402-1405-9 (pbk. : alk. paper)
   1. Compost. I. Title.
   S661.D38 2011
   635'.048975--dc22
                            2010035161

Acquisitions Editor, Candy Wiza
Edited by David Baker-Thiel
Designed by Clare Finney
Cover illustration by Melvyn Evans
Production coordinated by Mark Griffin

ABOUT THE AUTHOR

A graduate of the University of Illinois in Chicago, Stephanie Davies established her business, Urban Worm Girl, in 2008, and since then she has helped install hundreds of residential worm bins throughout the country. A Chicago resident, Stephanie hosts interactive lectures, demonstrations, and workshops on vermicomposting and various other forms of composting. Stephanie was a featured speaker at Green Festival in Chicago in 2009 and 2010, spreading the wisdom of the red wiggler worm and the environmental benefits of composting. She regularly speaks at schools, garden clubs, farmers markets, and within private homes. Stephanie and her worms have been featured in the *Chicago Tribune*, on ABC 7 in Chicago, Chicago's Progressive Talk radio, *Edible Chicago*, Library Life TV, and in many other newspapers and blogs. Along with her Urban Worm Girl colleague, Amber Gribben, Stephanie has been busy installing the first wave of commercial worm bins throughout Chicagoland to help manage commercial restaurant and office waste on a grand scale. In addition to being a sought-after vermiculture expert, Stephanie is an occupational therapist by trade. Through her diverse interests, she works to serve the planet and many of its inhabitants.

ACKNOWLEDGMENTS

There are few things we truly do alone in this world. Writing a book is definitely not one of them. The expertise, guidance, support, love, and loyalty of so many made it possible for me to complete this enormous endeavor. I am grateful to all of you. I am amazed that as you ask the universe for help, it so often answers in the form of new friends, family, and colleagues who are more than willing to lend a hand. Thank you universe, you never cease to amaze me!

I would like to express immeasurable thanks to my parents, Lillian and Larry Davies, for their lifelong support, encouragement, and patience. You both mean the world to me. A day does not pass without my awareness of the unique gifts you have both passed on to me.

A gigantic hug and kiss go out to you, Big Sis! Laurie, you are an amazing woman. Thank you for always leading this little sister in the right direction.

Many thanks to the compost community including, Dan (my favorite worm farmer), Lynn Bement "The Compost Queen", Seneca Kern, Angie (my favorite honorary worm girl), and most of all, thank you Amber Gribben, the other half of Urban Worm Girl. Your friendship, kindness, patience, incredible repertoire of organizational skills, ability to wrangle worms, and your photo and technical talent has kept me afloat for the last year. You have been an amazing addition to Urban Worm Girl and the world is a better place because of it!

Thank you, Leith Sharp, for your timely entrance into my life and your generous recommendations. Because of you, I have had the pleasure of working with Gretel Hakanson who has guided me through the thick and thin of this publication. Gretel, your skills are priceless.

I'd like to express special gratitude for the artists, photographers, and designers who have helped me to express my vision. Thank you Natalie Bianchi, John Bistolfo, Jon Hopfensperger, Shaun Rowe, and Valerie of Bark Design Chicago. Thank you, Becky Huinker, you captured the essence of my tiny ripe cherry tomato so well with your lens.

Gigantic bows and blessings to the emotional support team of Julie Brandies and Marian Baker. You have each added energy and hope back into this tired worm girl in very special ways.

In addition, I'd like to thank Candy Wiza, Annette Mambuca, and David Thiel for their professional expertise, direction, and support during this first-time publishing adventure.

Sincere gratitude to all the composting households and those about to bloom in the future.

DEDICATION

To Taz, the orange tabby cat of my dreams, who did his best to keep my lap warm on many chilly late nights. Thank you with all my heart for your loyalty and unconditional love. We had many beautiful days in the garden together.

Contents

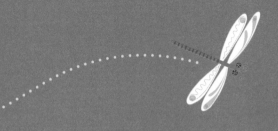

Preface: Inside & Out

Did you know that the art of composting can take place inside as well as outdoors? It's true: We can transform a great deal of our waste into compost in the confines of our homes. Within the pages of this book, you'll see that not only is indoor composting possible, but with a little guidance and few tools, it's quite simple. You'll also learn the best outdoor composting method for your unique living situation and the keys to success. You'll see the benefits of composting from some new perspectives, which occur both inside and out. Indoor houseplants fed compost burst forth with new growth and blooms, while the lawn outside your window will flourish, and the vegetable garden will produce its best tomatoes when fed compost.

There is no mistaking the benefits of the added biology and nutrients compost brings to indoor plants, gardens, soil, and the environment. But did you know that composting can also help you and your body inside and out? Taking on the activity of composting may have a transformative effect on both your inner and outer worlds, your mental well-being as well as your physical well-being. It has for me, and I wrote *Composting Inside & Out* to share my experience with you.

Physical Well-Being

The physical health benefits of compost are clear, especially if you plan to grow your own edibles. Compost provides nutrients, soil biology, and natural pest resistance, which leads to a happier and heartier garden without the use of harmful pesticides. Research shows that pesticides and chemical fertilizers used on lawns and gardens are absorbed into our bodies causing extensive health problems. These substances are stored in our cells and passed on to future generations. They also change the composition of the soil and the food grown in that soil, as well as the chemical makeup of the food, water, and air that we take into our bodies.

In an interview with *The Sun* magazine, Sandra Steingraber, an environmentalist and expert on the causes of cancer and reproductive problems, said, "other than the forty-six chromosomes bequeathed to us by our parents, we are simply rearranged molecules of air, food, and water." She reminds us of the obvious, "…you breathe in so many gallons of air every day; you drink so many quarts of water; and you eat so many molecules of food." Shouldn't it be clear upon hearing that reminder that we need to be very careful about what we ingest and to what we are exposed? Keeping chemicals, such as fertilizers and landfill leachate, out of our soil, air, and water is essential. Steingraber reminds us that the molecules you ingest and absorb daily, "…are knitted together to make your brain, your muscles, your hair, and your blood." The image of these toxic chemicals settling into the organs of your body can be quite disturbing. These are facts we can ignore no longer. To live happy and healthy lives, we need to change our agricultural habits, our waste management habits, and our reliance on chemicals. The small changes we make as individuals, such as composting instead of using landfills, have an effect not only on ourselves but also on all the life around us and our future generations.

Composting helps us understand and improve our diets and food habits. Although I am generally a healthy eater, composting with worms made me take notice of what I ate. The world around me became a list of items that were either organic, compostable waste or not. Waste became categorized as either worm food or not. With my eyes open and my attention to these details heightened, my diet improved even more. My grocery bags contained more and more veggies (which worms love) and less meats and processed foods (which harm worms). Worms should not be fed meats, cheeses, oils, vinegars and spices, including excessive salts, so I became more conscious of these items in my diet. If I ate these things, I could not feed them to my worms.

I would have to throw them in garbage, which would defeat my original intent of reducing my waste stream. As doctors have told us, we should be minimizing fatty and salty foods to ensure longevity and heart health. What's good for me is good for my worms. What feeds my compost feeds me, and now that I have a 10' × 4' (3m × 1m) raised bed full of organic edibles in my backyard, this principle carries even more meaning for me. My composted waste literally feeds my soil and my dinner plate.

When I began composting, I wasn't a strong gardener, and I had no plans to become one. But as composting increased my awareness of what I ate and where my food came from, I developed a longing to grow my own food and participate more fully in the cycles of life.

Mental Well-Being

As a healthcare provider for more than fifteen years, I can attest to the fact that our mental and emotional states also directly affect our physical health. Environmental factors are not the only concern. Medical research has documented the negative effect of stress on our bodies, and stress is a proven contributing factor to illness. Multitasking and complex lifestyles based on the ideas that "more is better" and "keeping up with the Joneses" are contributing to a culture of pain, disease, and illness. It is becoming more and more challenging to find time in our lives for simplicity and connection to the natural world. In a world that values convenience, multitasking, and productivity, it can be difficult to find joy associated with simpler times. Stopping to smell the roses, or in this instance, stopping to smell the compost, is more important than ever.

The art of composting, whether working with worms, Bokashi enzymes, or a traditional tumbler, allows us to experience a connection to the natural world and the cycle of life. The inner emotional and mental benefits may be a surprise to many. Reconnecting to textures of food, colors of soil, and smells of the earth feels good! An inner chord is struck when we see a beautiful ripe tomato on the vine, catch the whiff of a lily in bloom, or snack on a snap pea growing right in the yard. In that moment, all of life is complete; nothing is missing.

Often, floods of childhood memories return when I am caring for my worms or shoveling some fresh compost into the garden. As children, many of us were much freer, playing in the dirt, catching bugs, getting our hands dirty, and exploring the natural world around us. We actually saw the little creatures in the dirt and were curious about their existence. Those memories are candy for the brain, bringing back the sweet curiosity of youth and ease of living. If you haven't yet had the chance in life to experience these simple joys, it is never too late to start.

When reconnecting to the natural world, we are reminded of the Earth's inherent wisdom; we feel a little less worried about controlling all the details of the day. Natural forces are at work all around us supporting our needs. Just seeing this can feel like a sigh of relief. If we go a step further and nurture and support these natural forces with our discipline and energy, the process can be a joyful experience. It's joyful to spend time working for a greater good instead of caring only for ourselves, and that goodwill can extend to organisms we can barely see. Taking care of my compost microorganisms and my worms is different than caring for my orange tabby cat. In slowing down and taking the time necessary to care for these new working worms and soil organisms, I have gained new perspective. They are not exactly my companions, like my furry friend; they are my workers, stewards of the environment. Caring for them translates to caring for the creatures around me and caring for the planet. The extra time I take to cut up and wash food scraps that will easily and efficiently be processed by the organisms in my bin is service to the planet. Being open to the world around me and the role I play in its health has become a fulfilling priority. I hope it will do the same for you.

Housing and employing composting worms has enhanced my personal spiritual practice. I hope that *Composting Inside & Out* will enable you to explore how all forms of composting, including worm composting, enhances and nourishes your life on many varied levels. As individuals, we have choices to make every day about how we want to live our lives, and as anthropologist Margaret Mead stated, "Never doubt that a small group of thoughtful, committed citizens can change the world; indeed, it's the only thing that ever has." We are those thoughtful, committed citizens, and we can change the world! Restoring balance in our individual lives and our culture as a whole will take time. But now is the time to start. Be that change! Start composting today.

Introduction

It would be silly for me to deny that I was a tomboy grow-ing up. Not only did I have a subscription to *Ranger Rick* nature magazine, I also loved to get my hands in the dirt, wade in the creek, pick weed bouquets to sell to neighbors, build tree forts, and catch bugs that would scare my older sister. I held crawdaddy races, fabricated a set of cardboard wings to try to fly off the swing set, and memorized more than twenty birdcalls during hours of bird watching with my aunt Debbie. Did any of this translate into a green thumb as an adult or a lifetime dedicated to environmental activism? Maybe a career in flower arranging or ornithology? Not even close. I have spent the first twenty years of my adult life living in an urban jungle, in various small apartments and condos, working primarily in healthcare. How in the world did I become qualified to write this book about compost-ing? Good question. The same way that you will be able to compost wherever you may live and in whatever lifestyle you currently have—slowly and steadily, little by little, listening to the natural world around you like a child. Learn as you go. Seek out advice from elders and experts in the field. And, most importantly, enjoying getting your hands a little dirty again! Take my advice, I'm also the Urban Worm Girl!

1: Our Trash

"Life turns trash into land."

—Derrick Jensen and Aric McBay, *What We Leave Behind*

Nearly 250 million tons of municipal solid waste (MSW) was generated in the United States in 2008. That figure is in addition to significant amounts of glass, metals, and plastics that were sent to recycling facilities.[1] This abundance of material ends up in landfills. Most landfills are compacted so tightly that researchers have found twenty-five-year-old corncobs, grapes, and even complete newspapers that can still be read. These organic materials are perfectly compostable and biodegradable, and yet landfills are full of such items. Why aren't we composting it? It's obvious that we need to take a closer look at the way we dispose of our waste, especially our organic waste. The United States is the world's largest generator of waste; each American disposes of close to 4.5 pounds (2kg) of garbage per day!

Organic materials are the largest components of our trash and make up more than two-thirds of the solid waste stream.[2] In the context of waste and composting, organic material isn't necessarily chemical- or pesticide-free, like it is in the grocery store. Rather "organic" in this case refers to any material that contains carbon and nitrogen in varying proportions, such as food scraps, yard waste, paper, and manure. In the right environment, these organic materials would break down naturally over time. Unfortunately, a landfill is not the right environment.

Believe it or not, there was a period in U.S. history when there was no trash pickup, no landfills, and no dumps. Before mass production, technological advancement, and views on sanitation changed, things that we consider trash were saved, repurposed, and used to their full potential. Food scraps were fed to the animals, or they were composted and ultimately their nutrients were used to grow food. Even as late as 1842, an estimated ten thousand pigs wandered the streets of New York City eating discarded kitchen scraps thrown from windows and doors. This was an early form of waste management. Apparently it takes seventy-five pigs to eat one ton of garbage per day! Who knew? As our productivity increased and the amount and composition of our trash changed, we needed to develop methods to deal with it, and hence municipal trash service was born.

The practice of repurposing or reusing items was a natural inclination for our ancestors. Individuals creatively and practically made use of their leftovers and waste. They made rags out of old clothing instead of purchasing them; bones were used to make healthy soup, and

Each American disposes of close to 4.5 pounds of garbage per day!

neighbors even shared their organic waste to feed farm animals or used it to barter for manure to fertilize fields. Garbage had value. When did this change? Over time, as disposable products became more available and as trends changed in the automotive and fashion industries. Consumption increased, changing our definition of trash. The amount of garbage we

1. U.S. Environmental Protection Agency, "Organic Materials," www.epa.gov/osw/conserve/materials/organics/index.htm (accessed March 30, 2010).
2. Ibid.

produce and our need to have it removed has increased. Tools, appliances, and shoes used to be made to last and to be repaired. Today, it is usually cheaper to purchase a brand new item than have it repaired. For example, it's usually cheaper to get a new mobile phone (and even computer) than it is to replace the battery. And honestly, how many people do you know who use a cobbler to repair or replace a worn-out sole?

At some point, we stopped thinking about what was happening to our trash after it left the curb because it was transported out of sight. This distraction proved helpful to all those companies advertising more and better products to replace our old ones. Why look back at something old when we can look ahead toward something bigger and better? And so began our struggles with excessive consumption and our troubles with waste management!

HOW LANDFILLS WORK

Out of sight, out of mind. We dispose of something in a trash bin and never have to think of it again. Until recently, when recycling programs were widely implemented, most Americans functioned within this mindset. All discarded items ended up in dumps and landfills. These enormous piles of discarded stuff started accumulating at a breakneck pace. Organics, inorganics, chemicals, and hazardous industrial materials were all carried away from our homes and businesses and piled up or buried somewhere out of sight. Organized waste removal systems were designed to manage all of this garbage. Progress was upon us, or was it? Did the invention of landfills and the caravans of vehicles hired to fill them just delay the problems? We started storing trash in the depths of the Earth as well as on its surface. How long did we really think this would last? Like many other solutions viewed as progress, short-term gain outweighed long-term problems.

People realized that open dumps, the early version of landfills, were causing sickness in the community. Sanitary, or closed, landfills gradually caught on in the 1930s but got their biggest boost from the U.S. Army Corps of Engineers, which made sanitary landfills the disposal method of choice for military facilities during World War II.[3]

Today, a landfill is a large, outdoor site designed for the disposal of waste. There are different kinds of landfills that accept different materials.

Construction and demolition debris landfills accept only discarded building materials. Other types of landfills include industrial, hazardous waste and land-clearing debris. But generally, the trash and garbage that we throw away every day is disposed of in a municipal solid waste (MSW) landfill. Nationwide, the number of active MSW landfills has actually shrunk from nearly eight thousand in 1988 to 1,754 in 2007 according to the U.S. Environmental Protection Agency (EPA).[4] But what landfills lack in numbers is made up in size. Landfills are much bigger today than they were in the past. As such, today's landfills have a much longer lifespan and frequently accept waste from a much larger geographical area. Garbage is often trucked across state borders to come to rest in enormous designated sites.

MSW landfills have improved over time as problems began to arise. They now must be built in suitable geological areas away from fault lines, wetlands, flood plains, and other restricted areas. It eventually became important to protect ground water from the toxins filling these sites. The design of landfills now includes plastic liners and other materials like clay to prevent groundwater contamination from leachate.

When water percolates through the landfill, much like water through your coffeemaker, a soup of toxic chemicals, metals, pathogenic microorganisms, and organic matter is brewed. The resulting brew is leachate. Not only does this liquid build up over time and need to be managed but it also has the potential to leak out of landfills, harming our environment, our planet, and our health. The United States and the European Union now mandate the use of liners in landfills. In some cases, double liners are being used, which limits the likelihood of tears. Organic matter create liquid when it breaks down. If this liquid mixes with chemicals and toxins, it can create dangerous leachate. In this case, even the organics become part of the problem. The toxic chemical soup comprised of contaminated broccoli, potato peels, and

3. "Landfill 101," South Carolina DHEC Office of Solid Waste Reduction & Recycling, September 2009.

4. Ibid.

carrots no longer breaks down and nourishes the earth with nutrients. The contaminated matter pollutes the planet if free to seep into the soil.

Landfill operators must monitor leachate and test groundwater quality to determine if there is contamination. Landfill daily operation includes compacting and covering waste with several inches of soil or other material to reduce odor, and litter, and control rodents and pests. Closed landfills must have a final cover that includes a synthetic cap and a soil layer. Once the landfill is closed, the responsibility of the landfill operator doesn't end. Landfill operators must set aside funding to provide environmental protection during and after the closing of a landfill. In short, today's landfills are not completely safe and are expensive to design, build, and maintain. More

The Fresh Kills Landfill

The Fresh Kills Landfill in Staten Island, New York, is a troubled example. Many claim it is the world's largest landfill and the world's largest man-made structure. At its peak in 2001, twenty barges each carrying 650 tons of garbage were added daily. The landfill is twenty-five meters taller than the Statue of Liberty and its volume exceeds that of the Great Wall of China.[5] The landfill generated a great deal of controversy in part because it was unlined, causing thousands of pounds of toxic chemicals and heavy metals to leach in waterways.[6] The landfill has since been closed and is being transformed into a park.[7]

5. John Lloyd and John Mitchinson, *QI: The Book of General Ignorance*. (London: Faber and Faber, 2006).

6. Avi Adinyayev et. al., "Fresh Kills Landfill," CUNY Honors College at Brooklyn College, http://acc6.its.brooklyn.cuny.edu/~scintech/solid/silandfill.html (accessed April 2, 2010).

7. "Freshkills Park," New York City Department of Parks and Recreation, www.nycgovparks.org/sub_your_park/fresh_kills_park/html/fresh_kills_park.html (accessed March 30, 2010).

importantly, existing landfill capacity and space for new landfills is limited. Landfills also are subject to the not-in-my-backyard syndrome.

BIODEGRADABLE: AN AMERICAN MYTH

Leachate aside, what is the problem with throwing away biodegradable organic waste, such as banana peels, carrots, newspapers, and corncobs? They will all disappear eventually in the landfill, right? Wrong. Landfills are not designed to ensure that biodegradation occurs nor is their goal to unleash the nutrients within waste for use in soil preservation and enrichment. The modern design of a landfill is meant to be airtight and dry, an environment that creates a mummified version of our waste. This has the side effect of ensuring that corncobs last for decades, unable to breakdown. Biodegradable only refers to the *potential* of an item to breakdown; it does not guarantee it will break down.

Products that are described as *biodegradable* have the potential to breakdown in a safe and timely manner whereas *disposable* ones don't.[8] For example, the widely used and massively produced disposable polyethylene plastic bag may take close to a thousand years to break down, according to some scientists. Rather than biodegrade, these bags photodegrade—crack and break up into microscopic granules due to ultraviolet radiation—and, in the process, leave behind harmful chemicals. In truth, plastics bags have been around for only about fifty years, so we don't yet know how long they take to break down.[9]

Biodegradable implies a process that is possible but not necessarily guaranteed. A food item such as a corncob is officially biodegradable but it is not guaranteed to biodegrade (break down or decompose) if the environment is not conducive to the biodegrading process. The lack of microbes, moisture, and oxygen is what prevents the corncob from breaking down. Composting create the ideal conditions for biodegrading to occur. We need to continue to bridge the gap between biodegradable potential and the act of composting to allow organic waste to properly break down.

8. Look for the Biodegradable Products Institute (BPI) certification logo on products to ensure they are truly biodegradable and compostable.

9. Juliet Lapidos, "Will My Plastic Bag Still Be Here in 2507?", *Slate*, www.slate.com/id/2169287/ (accessed April 2, 2010).

At this point, you may be wondering: What's the difference between composting and biodegrading? Composting is an art or a practice. It is creating the environment necessary for biodegradation to happen. When organic items break down or decompose with the help of microbes, we are rewarded with the dark, rich, earthy substance known as compost. Organic materials suitable for this process (and, therefore, *compostable*) include: food scraps such as apple cores, banana peels, vegetable waste; coffee grounds; tea bags; yard waste; paper and plain brown cardboard (not printed or waxed); and many animal manures. Composting is the process that ensures that biodegradation occurs. It is the purposeful, intentional activity in a clearly defined environment controlled or monitored by us with the purpose of releasing the value in the items we compost.

Corn-based BioBags made without polyethylene, are compostable and, therefore, biodegradable. According to the manufacturer, they "will decompose in a controlled composting environment in ten to forty-five days, leaving no harmful residues behind" when in the right conditions.[10] The key here is the right conditions! As we have learned, today's dry, anaerobic landfills do not have the right conditions for this type of process to occur.

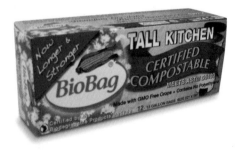

Courtesy of BioBag USA

Though using these types of bags may seem like a nice alternative to plastic bags, are we making a difference if they are being thrown into landfills filled with our nutrient-rich organic scraps?

Man-made compostable and biodegradable products, such as BioBags are only helpful when used with a conscious composting effort. They can make it easier to collect organic waste and cleanly deliver it to a compost bin or facility where the material will eventually fully biodegrade under carefully monitored conditions. But these bags aren't a substitute for composting. Biodegradable products are not the answer to our excessive garbage problem. They will not extend the life of landfills or solve the problem of limited space. Only a change in our waste management will

10. "Bio Bag Fact," Bio Bag USA, http://www.biobagusa.com/ (accessed April 13, 2010).

solve this problem. Organic materials should be diverted to a compost pile or municipal composting facility, where available, instead of a landfill.

WATCHING OUR WASTE

Composting is a growing solution to our solid waste management problems. According to the EPA, the amount of waste that has been diverted from landfill disposal through composting has *quadrupled* since 1990, from 2 percent of total MSW to 8.4 percent today. In fact, 62 percent of all yard trimmings are composted in more than 3,500 municipal yard trimming composting programs in the United States and twenty-three states ban at least some organics disposal in landfills, mostly leaves, grass and other yard debris.

An increasing number of municipalities are developing curbside pickup composting programs in an effort to reduce the amount of material sent to landfills. In 2004, the City and County of San Francisco rolled out a "three-stream" (compostables, recyclables, and trash) curbside program.

Today, throwing away compostable material, such as banana peels and apple cores, can result in a fine for both homeowners and businesses, as city law actually requires composting. Compostable materials are collected in green toter carts and include all food scraps, food-soiled paper, and yard trimmings. Instead of being taken to a landfill, four hundred tons of compostable material is delivered each day to a facility where it is converted into a nutrient-rich soil amendment. The resulting compost is then used to produce the organic food and wine that San Francisco is famous for. Since the program's inception, landfill waste has been reduced by more than 24 percent.[11] Other cities have developed similar programs and yet the majority of our cities lack this option for their residents. Residents are left to make choices regarding their organic waste disposal. The choice should be composting.

The amount of waste that has been diverted from landfill disposal through composting has *quadrupled* since 1990.

Composting is an easy and fun way to reduce the trash that you send to the landfill. And it can have a significant impact because 35 percent of your household waste can be diverted from landfills through composting. As you move toward a composting future, try to shift your perspective from convenience to mindfulness. A shift is far overdue. We can start with redefining our waste or garbage and becoming more aware of its inherent value.

As a healthcare provider, I have had many conversations with patients about their definitions of pain. Without lacking compassion, I invite my patients to redefine pain in as many ways as possible. Contrary to what one might expect, instead of spiraling further into the pain, this activity can help to unlock frustrations and restore a sense of freedom and hope from a seemingly endless struggle. Pain is not one thing; it is many various sensations. We can use and work with some of these sensations to ease the pain and create comfort. Similarly, as we redefine garbage, we find out it is a rich, diverse world of valuable materials. We may find answers in this

11. "Composting," SFEnvironment, www.sfenvironment.org/our_programs/topics.html?ti=6 (accessed April 2, 2010).

waste and encourage new life in an old system. Small shifts in our perspectives and the language we use build new possibilities that expand our world. Organic garbage is rich with unused nutrients and willing to give them back to us. It is not to be discarded without thought.

The word "trash" didn't even exist until 1518. At that time, it was used to describe "anything of little use or value." It originates from the Middle English and Old Norse words for fallen leaves and twigs: "trasch" and "tros." The term came to describe domestic garbage in 1906. Perhaps that implies there was no trash before 1518, which makes sense when you consider that trash does not occur in nature. It's as if the very words, "trash" and "garbage" have no reference in our natural world. Nature operates in a system where the needs of millions of species are met without producing any waste. Unused or excreted materials are food for other organisms and returned to the soil as we will see in the next chapter.

2: Our Soil

"I want to touch the earth, I want to rake it in my hands, I want to grow something wild and unruly."

—The Dixie Chicks

Our soil is alive, and like all living things, it can become sick or even die. The results of which are tragic for all living creatures, including us! Our health and well-being and the health and well-being of the entire food chain is clearly linked to the health of our soil. In addition to our sprawling urban landscapes and natural habitat destruction, regular plowing and spraying of chemical pesticides and fertilizers is severely damaging our soil and the living creatures within and on top of it.

The living creatures that dwell in soil decompose naturally occurring organic matter. This is nature's way of taking care of the soil. This natural balancing process has become interrupted by modern agricultural practices. Composting is our way to help Mother Nature complete this essential job and, therefore, return the nutrients that we take from her. Our composting habits not only benefit our personal gardens and reduce excessive landfill waste, but these efforts can also quickly change the health of the earth's covering, nourish the creatures under the surface, and support our increasing need for healthy soil, not to mention expand our circle of friends. There is a composting community out there waiting to support you.

NOT ALL SOIL IS THE SAME

Soil is the loose upper layer of the earth's surface and is made of varying amounts of sand, silt, clay, and organic matter. Good garden soil that promotes plant growth is very valuable to us as humans. The value is not only based on our desire to have beautiful gardens but to maintain our agricultural needs (our food), prevent natural disasters such as landslides and forest fires, and even to enhance our immune systems (healthy soil means healthy food).

Good garden soil is made up of 30 to 50 percent sand, 30 to 50 percent silt, 20 to 30 percent clay, and 5 to 10 percent organic matter (humus). The organic matter in soil is its life! Soil that has been abused over time through mass agricultural efforts and chemical runoff or left standing in urban sprawl is sick or starving. The organic material content in much of our soil today is minimal to absent. The life has literally been drained out of it. Left alone, this soil will continue to die. With help from our composting efforts, it can once again thrive and provide us with nature's beauty and abundance. We can bring the soil back to life.

SOIL HEALTH

Our planet's soil health is an ever-increasing ecological concern. Environmentalists have been researching it for years. Soil health refers to the soil's capacity to function as a vital living system. The number of and diversity of living organisms within the soil are its lifeblood, and also an indication of the life (plants and vegetables) the soil may eventually produce.

The Earth's topsoil carries a heavy load of responsibility. Though it is merely the first 2 inches (5cm) of the earth's surface, its job is enormous. When healthy, topsoil manages water flow, water retention and decomposition of organic matter; it maintains the structure (architecture) and texture of our planet, and it helps to process and distribute nutrients necessary for plant life. It contains vital nutrients that help plants grow strong roots and gives the roots something on which to anchor. Healthy soil acts like a policing force, fighting the bad guys (bad bacteria and pests) by the suppression of pathogens and toxins that invade the environment. Fighting the endless number of toxins entering our environment today is a full time job for this soil. The importance of its function cannot be minimized or overlooked and yet it frequently is. Soil scientist John Doran wrote, "… the thin layer of soil covering the surface of the earth represents the difference between survival and extinction for most land based life."[1]

Permaculture

A blend of two words, "permanent" and "agriculture," permaculture is a concept initially developed in the 1960s by Austrian farmer Sepp Holzer. After taking over the family farm, Holzer began applying new ecologically based methods to his growing. He was attempting to mimic the natural ecosystems around him and was working with the existing interconnections of the living earth. These successful and less damaging methods of agriculture proved to be beneficial for Holzer and his land. Following nature's models, including maintaining biodiversity in his planting methods, allowed Holzer to successfully farm the same land for more than forty-five years!

Though most who stumble upon modern-day permaculture ideas are exposed to it through exploration of gardening or agricultural methods, it now incorporates many disciplines including architecture, industrial design, and education. The theory of permaculture was further developed by Australians, Bill Mollison and David Holmgren in the early 1970s. Their work pointed out the

Clearly, changes in the structure and content of soil and the depletion of soil leads to severe problems. The implications of this are far reaching. For example, soil erosion is touted as a major cause of natural disasters, such as landslides, and atmospheric pollutants. Loose, dry, dead soil is carried away easily. This soil erosion could also lead to the inability of agriculture to sustain the survival of humans and other creatures on the planet. Yet, it is widely believed that we have already lost close to a third of our topsoil in just the last hundred years! At this rate, we are in grave danger of losing the remaining source of our planet's fertility.

Soil is a requirement for human life, however, all over the world, we have neglected soil's needs in the pursuit of practices such as mechanical

1. John W. Doran, "Soil Health and Global Sustainability: Translating Science Into Practice," *Agriculture, Ecosystems & Environment* 88, no. 2 (2002).

inherent efficiency of Mother Nature and her diverse worker population. By employing all creatures to work together, she can harness the planet's energies and recycle the fruits of their labor with minimal to no loss.

Mollison and Holmgren turned our eyes to nature. These two men also expanded the notions applied to agriculture to include many more aspects of human behavior and lifestyle. Permaculture uses a set of core values for all situations: "Earth's care," "people care," and "fair share." By employing these values, we are reminded to nurture planet Earth (Earth care), our relationships to each other (people care) as well as our need to limit over consumption for the long-term health and productivity of the planet (fair share). Educational programs and permaculture communities are popping up worldwide. Not only are people coming together with a shared vision for today and future generations, they are rebuilding their connections to nature and the creatures that make up its biodiversity.

Various methods of composting are employed throughout permaculture design projects. It is not the actual composting that is an essential permaculture design component, rather it is the strength of the relationships inherent in composting. There is power and resources in building a relationship between our waste, our yards and gardens, and our food sources. In addition, getting connected to Earth's soil and the microorganisms in the soil builds a healthy platform for our future generations.

cultivation or mass rototilling. This process releases carbon dioxide and kills the soil's food web—the interconnected community of small organisms that maintain its balance. We have spent too much time looking to maximize production above the surface and have neglected the threads of life below the surface. This intricate network of creatures determines the life of the soil. The strategies associated with mass agriculture literally wear out the soil, its inhabitants and its physical structure. In addition to killing our most valuable team members, we are damaging our atmosphere with our agricultural methods. As these essential microorganisms are broken down and disrupted, they release carbon dioxide, which is also a major contributor to global warming. According to Ron Amundson, Ph.D. at UC Berkeley, 20 percent of the CO_2 getting into the atmosphere is directly or indirectly coming from agricultural plowing.

 There is nothing quite like the smell of "earth" in all its glory.

For the future of our soil's health, our health, and our future generations' health, we must conserve our existing soil as well as learn how to nurture and enhance it!

HUMUS: THE KEY TO SOIL HEALTH

Although soil is made of several components—silt, clay, sand, water, air, and organic matter or humus—the presence of humus is the primary factor for determining its health. The humus content literally gives life to the soil and its many inhabitants, feeding them and allowing them to release nutrients for the surrounding plant life.

Humus is essentially the organic matter in the soil that is in the process of breaking down. This organic matter is made up of a combination of leaves, twigs, insect remains, food scraps, plant hulls and stems, leftover vegetation, and manure. As all of this matter begins to break down with the help of soil microbiology, the color, texture, and smell are transformed. In general, humus is dark and rich in color; it often has a spongy texture and a sweet earthy smell (not the actively decaying or ripe smell of a compost heap or pile). There is nothing quite like the smell of earth in all of its glory. Humus is just that.

The most nutrient rich stage of humus is "active" or "effective" humus. In this initial stage, the nutrients are readily available for most plant roots to access. The benefits are immediate yet the humus can continue to break down further, resulting in long-term benefits for soil health. Eventually the humus becomes "stable" or "passive." The soil microbes have transformed it, creating the perfect texture for water retention and drainage, airflow, and plant root penetration and support. Because stable humus can hold approximately 80 percent of its weight in water, it has drought resistant properties. This significantly reduces its likelihood for erosion and natural disaster in addition to increasing its growing potential. Humus is no longer being broken down at the stable stage and has been estimated to last thousands of years in the soil.

Humus is referred to as the cornerstone of soil. Its makeup and percentage of presence affects all aspects of the soil and is in turn affected by all aspects. Healthy garden soil benefits from a humus content of at least 5 percent. We need to care for the humus content of our soil to support the food chain and the balance of Earth's ecosystem.

Without the cornerstone to soil life, our very existence will be threatened. Composting our waste returns the life to our soil through organic matter or humus content. The best scenario for optimum soil health is a combination of active and stable humus to support the various stages and needs of agriculture. Unfortunately, most agricultural operations do not replenish soil. Composting can immediately address this widespread problem.

"IT'S ALIVE!"

In addition to being made up of minerals and particulate matter, healthy soil also contains living creatures. This diverse array of creatures, when they are left to do their jobs, makes the job of growing healthy food easy. They perform various duties, including processing, moving, and storing nutrients, acting as the glue to help hold the particles of our soil together as well as aerate the actual body of soil as the creatures move through it. When kept in balance, this army of critters even regulates pathogens, harmful bacteria and fungi in our soil, keeping disease and pests to a minimum.

These hardworking creatures are underappreciated and often purposefully ignored or even sought after and killed! Chemical fertilizers and pesticides and other toxic waste and landfill leachate wreak havoc on them. Keeping these creatures alive is essential to keeping our soil, our plants, and once again ourselves, alive. Some of the beneficial creatures found in healthy soil include:

- several yards of fungi per teaspoon
- more than a billion bacteria per teaspoon
- several thousand protozoa per teaspoon
- multitudes of insects, including springtails, mites, beetles, spiders
- up to fifty earthworms per square foot

Soil Loss

Soil erosion is as big an environmental problem as global warming, according to scientists.[2] The surface of the earth is essential for the production of our nutrients, and it is disappearing rapidly. One soil scientist says topsoil is our number one export.[3] As loose, dry, lifeless soil is blown or washed away, it lands in our waterways and is carried off or builds up in lakes, rivers, and streams. Both its absence on land and the buildup in the water are problematic. The build up of soil in waterways creates unnatural circumstances in aquatic habitats, smothering plant and animal life and eliminating valuable food sources.

Though erosion is a natural process, the rate of erosion is rapidly increasing due to destructive activities. Deforestation leaves the soil exposed and vulnerable. Mass industrial agriculture depletes the soil, leaving it lifeless. Urban sprawl covers or pollutes what space we have left. Research states that modern farming techniques increase erosion ten to forty times the natural rate.[4] Yet nature generates new topsoil extremely slowly—it takes around five hundred years for nature to produce an inch of topsoil.

It is up to us to slow down soil erosion. Realizing we are contributing to soil erosion with presently accepted agricultural methods is a start. For every unit of food we consume, using the conventional agricultural methods employed in the United States, six units of topsoil are lost.[5]

An additional benefit to regenerating dry and lifeless soils with our rich compost is its value in preventing further soil erosion. Healthy soil contains just the right amount of organic matter to maintain the balance needed to keep soil resilient. The strength of

These bacteria, insects, and fungi are often targeted as culprits of our failed growing attempts. This couldn't be further from the truth. A lost crop of tomato plants may be due to a complex array of soil imbalances, leading to increased plant vulnerability, not just the presence of a harmful bacteria, fungi, or insects. In fact, researchers discovered that exposure to soil early in a human's life can even reduce cardiovascular disease as an adult.[6] They also seem to support our immune systems as suggested in the recent research. It is essential to understand the interconnections and networks of underground life that team up to support our growing needs

6. Robert Channick "NU Study: Dirt's Good for Kids," *Chicago Tribune*, March 24, 2010, www.chicagotribune.com/health/ct-x-n-health-dirt-20100324,0,6756958.story (accessed March 31, 2010).

the soil structure and the life that maintains that structure is less likely to be affected by wind and water erosion but it is porous enough to allow water to percolate through to the plant roots held at varying levels within.

A balanced composition of silt, sand, clay, and organic matter allows air and nutrients to move freely and nourish plants and the soil creatures tending to them. A balanced composition also helps retain moisture, much like a sponge, which allows a protective layer of plants to grow. This extra layer of plant covering enhances the safety of the soil and feeds the soil organisms. Like creating a balanced meal, we can eliminate or add ingredients to our soil to modify its makeup and encourage strength. Compost enables us to put nutrients and organic matter back into the soil's composition, strengthening it against natural and human-imposed stresses.

2. Tim Radford, "Soil Erosion As Big a Problem As global warming, say scientists," *The Guardian*, February 14, 2004, www.guardian.co.uk/world/2004/feb/14/science.environment (accessed April 27, 2010).

3, 4 & 5. Larry Gallagher, "The Joy of Dirt," *Ode Magazine*, March 2010, www.odemagazine.com/doc/69/dirt (accessed April 27, 2010).

on this planet. Many of these soil creatures are the same creatures we will recruit in our composting efforts. We can't do it without them!

Even though many of the life forms in our soil are actually too small to see with the naked eye, they are numerous and perform massive amounts of work. For example, bacteria outnumber all other organisms present in soil. Scientists estimate that 250,000 to 500,000 bacteria would fit in the period at the end of this sentence and that a billion bacteria reside in a teaspoon of good soil. These ancient organisms are the primary decomposers of the natural waste on the surface of the forest floor. "Without [bacteria] we would be smothered in our own waste in a matter of months," authors Jeff Lowenfels and Wayne Lewis wrote in their book *Teaming with Microbes: A Gardeners Guide to the Soil Food Web*.

In addition to decomposing waste, bacteria are experts at storing nutrients that are have been ingested by other beings in the food chain, including plant life. As they ingest organic wastes, they process and then subsequently hold these valuable nutrients in their structure for later use. When the bacteria die, they then deposit the nutrients back into the soil. But usually bacteria get a bad name. Of course, we have all heard of the negative characteristics of pathogenic bacteria, such as E-coli. These harmful bacteria tend to live in anaerobic (without oxygen) environments such as the intestinal tract. Beneficial bacteria breed in aerobic (with oxygen) environments. In a balanced soil, the harmful bacteria are kept in control by the beneficial bacteria. Maintaining balance is Mother Nature's forte; we have so much to learn from her. There is no need to target these harmful strains of bacteria when we are able to support the balance in the soil.

If the presence and function of bacteria is not enough reason to take better care of our dirt, then wait until you learn a bit more about fungi! The fungi most widely recognized are mushrooms and toadstools, but most fungi are microscopic. There are more 100,000 different kinds of fungi, and fungi experts suspect there are millions more still to be discovered. Fungi create extensive networks, or strand systems, under our feet. As a result of these systems, tunnels form to allow water and nutrient flow from deep in the soil up to the surface where plant roots can find them. Some plants actually lure fungi to their root systems to ensure that they have a constant supply of food. Once again Mother Nature never ceases to amaze! Much like bacteria, these fungi also work hard to decompose the waste on the surface of the Earth. Unlike bacteria, who prefer softer, greener, nitrogen-based diets, fungi prefer heavier, woodier materials. The two are a match made in heaven, a perfect team! Within a compost pile, they work together to break down all the various textures we give them.

Deemed as a nuisance by some, insects, bacteria, and fungi are essential to soil health. Our composting efforts, as you will soon see, nourish these residents of the soil. Everything in nature has a purpose—including such creatures—and everything in nature is designed to work synergistically to sustain life on earth. Supporting our soils with added humus from our composting efforts will make a tremendous difference in the longevity and quality of our soil. Yet if we continue to add harsh chemicals and toxins (present in many pesticides) to our lawns and gardens in attempts to control and manage so called "pests," we will continue a killing cycle.

When we choose to apply pesticides to our garden and lawn to minimize weeds and pests, we are actually killing many of the living organisms we need along with the targeted pests. These chemicals not only cause harm to our network of workers in the soil, they also leach through the soil and end up in our water systems creating even more damage.

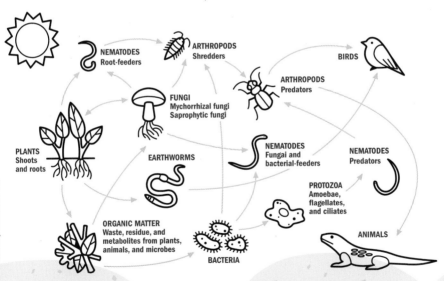

Illustration by Michelle Shi

Soil food web: primary, secondary and tertiary organisms transforming organic waste. (Modified from Soil Foodweb, Inc. www.soilfoodweb.com)

Not only does this damage affect us, it also affects our offspring. In 2004, researchers from two major laboratories performed a study to analyze the presence of toxic chemicals in umbilical cord blood of newborn babies born in U.S. hospitals. Many of the 287 chemicals detected in umbilical cord blood were pesticides.[7]

"Artificial fertilizers lead to artificial nutrition, artificial animals, and finally to artificial me," said Albert Howard, a British agronomist and botanist who lived in the early 1900s and is now hailed as the founder of the organic farming movement. This gives us something to consider in regards to the food we eat and its effect on the internal environment of our bodies.

In addition to the presence of toxins in ourselves and our children, nitrogen laden chemical fertilizers are so widely used that their runoff has created an enormous "dead zone" in the Gulf of Mexico. We are actually fertilizing the gulf through enormous applications of these fertilizers. The source is not only large industrial farms but also our individual lawn maintenance strategies. After these fertilizers make their way through the rivers and streams to the Gulf, they encourage extensive algae blooms that would not naturally occur. These blooms eventually drain off the oxygen in the lower levels of the Gulf, subsequently starving the bottom life. Once again, rather than helping, our poor choices in soil management and amendments take their toll on the natural world and our food sources in the ocean. Implementing organic farming and gardening practices will minimize these deadly affects. Some cities and towns have realized the effects of pesticides and are starting to take action. For example, Marblehead, Massachusetts, was the first U.S. municipality to ban lawn pesticides on public property, and other cities and towns are following suit.

NOTHING GOES TO WASTE

We have much to learn from the ecosystem under our feet. The wonders of Mother Earth and her natural recycling system are a perfect model for solving problems related to our over-consumption. Nothing goes to waste in healthy soil. There is no garbage in nature, only the garbage that we impose. The living organisms in healthy soil process the organic leftovers,

7. E. Galen, "Study Finds Hundreds of Toxic Chemicals in Umbilical Cords of Newborns," World Socialists Web Site, www.wsws.org/articles/2005/dec2005/toxi-d07.shtml (accessed March 19, 2010).

Biomimicry

Biomimicry is the "science and art of emulating nature's best biological ideas to solve human problems."[8] The most famous example of biomimicry is the invention of Velcro. The Swiss engineer who invented Velcro noticed that the end of each piece of dog hair has a tiny hook, which causes it to stick to anything with a loop such as clothing (as most of us have clearly seen). Velcro, of course consists of a strip of hooked material and an opposite strip of a loose-looped material

that holds the hooks.[9] As Janine Benyus, pioneer of the biomimicry movement and author of the 1997 book, *Biomimcry: Innovation Inspired by Nature* states, "The more our world functions like the natural world, the more likely we are to endure on this home that is ours, but not ours alone." Composting and other organic growing and lawn care methods are examples of biomimicry because they follow nature's examples of pace and overall respect for fellow creatures.

8. Biomimicry Institute, "Why Biomimicry?", www.biomimicryinstitute.org/ (accessed March 31, 2010).
9. Brainz, "The 15 Coolest Cases of Biomimicry," http://brainz.org/15-coolest-cases-biomimicry/ (accessed March 31, 2010).

scraps, and carcasses of other dead organisms and plants. This ensures that nutrients remain in the soil and are passed on to the plants and vegetables growing above. This is a part of the soil food web. This term and its surrounding theories have helped establish a better understanding of nature's form of recycling and composting. The concepts behind the soil food web show the value of interconnection and working as a team with the soil and its inhabitants. Like many things, we don't need to reinvent the wheel; nature can show us the healthiest and most efficient ways to do many things.

SOIL TESTING

So how do we know how our soil has been treated? How long do the effects of chemicals last? Can our compost fix it right away? There are many serious gardeners who test their soils before beginning a vegetable or flower garden to find out just what they are starting with. Typically, soil testing involves mailing a sample of soil to a lab that specializes in soil testing. Often, a local university will have an extension program that offers soil testing. The cost varies depending on the complexity of the procedure, but most start around twenty dollars. The information provided will vary depending on your specific requests. Soil testing can target pH, organic matter content, and trace minerals, as well as the presence of metals and other toxins. If requested, some facilities will provide recommendations based on the results as well. The average gardener may not be able to easily interpret the lab results. An advanced knowledge of soil science could be required. If needed, find a master gardener in your area to help you work through the, sometimes complicated results of a soil test. Having said this, testing will provide a baseline, which will be helpful for your working information. It will also help you build your vocabulary and knowledge about soil, its makeup, and its web of organisms.

In general, I find that most home gardeners may want to explore their own soil content. This provides a clearer understanding of the texture and growing capacity of the structure of your soil. A simple in-home test, which will help identify what type of soil you have, can be useful in determining what will grow best in your soil. Do you have lighter, sandier soil, or heavy clay-based soil? In addition, performing this home soil test

will get your hands in the dirt and start to familiarize you with the variations in texture, color, and smell of dirt. As you become more familiar with the qualities of soil, you will inevitably be drawn to the obvious benefits that compost can provide. Its rich, dark, aromatic nature just looks and feels ready to burst with flowers, fruits, and vegetables. Whether your test reveals that your soil is heavy or light, compost is the answer. It helps to balance out the water retention and filtration properties as well as the air flow in the soil.

You don't need much to begin your home soil test. Just follow the simple directions below:

1. Find a large jar with a lid. Clean it out thoroughly making sure there is no sticky residue left.

2. Go out into your yard and find an undisturbed area with a light covering of natural debris on top. Don't choose a heavily gardened area for this test. If you have added fertilizers or soil amendments to the area, you will not get an accurate reading of your native soil.

3. Clear the surface debris off and cut a slice of soil about 6" to 8" (15cm–20cm) deep, with the same width at the top and the bottom (like a large slice of chocolate cake).

4. Place this in the jar and fill it with water. Once the soil is covered with water, replace the lid and shake vigorously until all of the soil is saturated with water. If you still see large clumps of soil floating in the jar, wait an hour and shake again.

5. Once the contents of the jar have fully dissolved in the water, set it somewhere to settle for twenty-four hours. Choose a place where there will be enough of a light source to peer through the contents without needing to disturb the jar.

6. Now just wait. When you return after a day, you will see that the soil particles have separated into their individual components.

This procedure will create layers based on the weight of the particles, which will allow you to see the composition of your soil. Gravel and small stones will be the bottom level, the next layer will be comprised of sand, followed by silt (pulverized sand particles), clay will be sitting on top of this, and then any organic matter will be at the very surface. This will give you a basic visualization right away. If you are so inclined to find out the actual percentages of these layers making up your soil, you can go one step further and opt for the laboratory testing.

The value of healthy soil is becoming clearer to us each day. Our dwindling supply of fertile soil leaves all creatures, including ourselves, vulnerable. Composting will nourish our fellow citizens under the surface as well as sustain our larger home, Mother Earth. This is just one of our responsibilities as citizens on the planet.

3: Becoming A Composter

"Put your hands into the earth. Live close to the ground."

—Wendell Berry

Modern day humans did not invent the science of composting. Actually, in the last 150 years, we have forgotten the natural way the earth decomposes its (and our) waste. Age-old composting practices revolved around organizing growing areas where the valuable resources of animal manure and organic waste were piled. Our ancestors knew how to maximize gains in the garden and how to utilize all of their waste. In modern times, we seem to value convenience over quality, short-term benefits over future gains, and technology over nature. With a bit of effort and education, we can once again be stewards of the earth and participate in the cycles of life and the cycles of the soil.

We have invented synthetic fertilizers in an attempt to mimic the benefits of composted waste. Many of us drive to the store to pick up a bag or two of fertilizer because we think it takes less time than collecting our waste and creating our own compost. Though it may be more immediate, is it really more convenient? And is it worth it in the long run? The environmental impact of the chemicals in these products alone proves that it is not. The carbon footprint created in making and delivering these products, even the organic ones, should also be considered. How far are these products traveling to get to your backyard? What energy output went into their production? Your kitchen scraps are not only nutrient rich, they are as local as it gets! And what about the loss of all that waste itself? The valuable compostable materials we call garbage become waste in the true sense of the word, carted off to a landfill to sit for years to come. Their value, "trashed." Chemical fertilizers are fabricated to do the job of humus and organic matter, which occur in nature without our help and are also created through the composting process.

It can be argued that it is not our fault. We follow the rules we were taught by our parents; "clean up after yourself," we were told time and again. As creatures of habit, most of us don't think twice about an alternative option to our garbage can. Where else would we put those stinky, slimy leftovers long forgotten in the back of the refrigerator or the tough unpalatable stalks of asparagus? The idea of placing animal, vegetable, and even human waste in the ground to compost is not archaic or out of date, it's natural genius in action. The cycle of life and the interconnectedness of all beings is perfected in this simple act.

The recognition of the declining state of our soil and the obvious negative effects our human behaviors have on the environment will naturally lead to the desire to make changes. This change can take the form of new behaviors, such as composting and recycling. The effort needed to make change originates from an increased sense of personal responsibility and value placed on simple, natural methods and the obvious intelligence of Mother Earth. This effort is priceless and can vastly improve the environment around and within us.

COMPOST REWARDS

Compost has rewards beyond our imagination. We benefit specifically in our gardens and, less obviously, within our thinking. Finished compost contributes to flourishing gardens because it contains most of the nutrients that plants need to grow, including boron, manganese, iron, copper, and zinc. These essential elements are not often found in chemical fertilizers. Furthermore, using compost on our gardens actually returns to the soil what we have been taking away from it for years, the nutrients of life. The use of compost on our lawns and gardens benefits all beings. In one application, we can minimize the toxic effects of commercially produced fertilizers, maximize nutrient absorption, and give soil the life it needs to continue to maintain our lives on this planet.

In addition to life-giving nutrients, compost has obvious additional benefits for the garden. It increases soil's capacity to hold water for future use by plants and it enhances the structure of the soil. For example, dry, thin soil is significantly more vulnerable to wind erosion. Michael Pollan notes in his book, *Second Nature*, "one hundred (45kg) pounds of humus (the main constituent of compost) can hold one hundred and ninety pounds of water!" This amazing capacity builds the functionality of soil for plant health and vigor as well as soil's resistance to the environmental impacts of wind erosion.

 Bugs become friends, worms become our teammates, and bacteria and fungi become our partners in the process of enhancing the soil.

Humus helps bind sand, clay, and silt particles together, locking in water and nutrients. Therefore, compost increases soil's resistance to drought and as a bonus, humus-rich soil leads to less watering. Less watering may indeed lead to savings in your water bill as well as saving our natural resources.

Can composting encourage you to see the world differently? Many compost converts have told me that it has done so for them, and I have to admit it has changed my perspective as well. This is where the surprise may come. How can separating and collecting our waste change how we see the world?

Contributing to the greater good of all makes a difference in our perspective in life. Seeing the bigger picture can only enhance our level of satisfaction here on earth. Knowing the good that we are doing beyond our own personal needs is a beautiful reward in and of itself. Our perspective also changes when we embark on new behaviors like composting. Learning new behavior requires care and commitment. It opens our eyes to the larger world around us, much like a child seeing things fresh.

To succeed in new behaviors, we must be observers and students once again. Bugs become friends, worms become our teammates, and bacteria and fungi become our partners in the process of enhancing the soil. When we change our perspectives, our view of the world changes as well. Whether those slimy, spineless, blind, deaf, and toothless soil creatures, like the worm, really influence us when we house them in our compost bins, or whether we just learn from our choices, the world becomes full of miraculous moments. There is nothing like watching garbage transform into soil or getting a whiff of fresh and fertile compost as you rake through it with your fingers. Dedicated composters begin categorizing everyday materials around them in terms of "worm food" and "nonworm food" in a very short time! The new physical form of garbage as dark black soil becomes a treat to work through your fingers and something to look forward to feeling at the end of a long day at the office. The stresses of everyday life are often forgotten as we turn our attention outwards to the compost bin and the garden soil. Who would have thought we could care for ourselves, the soil, and the entire ecosystem so easily?

In my experience, one of the hardest things to convince people of is that a commitment to the future (the big picture) is essential to good health. Being shortsighted and fixing problems as they arise are not healthful qualities; building a healthy lifestyle plan and staying committed are. When my physical rehabilitation clients begin a stretching and strengthening program, they often ask, "Am I ever going to be able to stop doing this now that I've started?" The answer is "no." A strong and flexible, healthy body needs tending to. The same is true of our dedication to composting and its effects on our soil. Just like stretching our tight and tense muscles, we observe with composting that once we are committed and see the results of our efforts, we can't go back. Our behavior and knowledge have changed forever, changing our influence on the planet!

THE TEAM APPROACH

I suspect that many feel overwhelmed by the thought of taking on one more project or learning one more skill. I have heard this from many family members and close friends, even those who are environmentally conscious individuals. It is true that a new skill may take a bit of time to learn but don't worry about perfecting it, composting is a forgiving art. You can do it less than perfectly and still reap its benefits. It should be shaped and developed to fit your tastes and your specific life. Of course, there are some tools of the trade, essential starting points, and basic procedures (which are explained in detail in chapters 5 and 6).

There's no need to feel overwhelmed or alone in your efforts to begin composting. Not only are there ample resources out there to help guide you in your efforts, there are a team of critters who are happy to do most of the work. This enthusiastic hard-working team of bacteria, fungi, worms, and insects carry the load and take care of many of the details. We just have to invite them in. Change is possible once we decide to embark on it.

BEGIN AT THE BEGINNING

In the words of the self-professed "Compost Queen," from Chicago, Lynn Bement, "Just start composting!" Though there are choices to make, equipment to purchase, and things to learn, there is no reason you can't compost in some form. To begin, start thinking of yourself as one of "them!" One of those environmentally-savvy composters you have heard about. Whether you are an urban dweller like myself, a suburban resident, or a rural landowner, composting is possible for everyone at some level, from an indoor worm compost, to a large outdoor heap, or backyard tumblers. It just takes a change of habits.

A new purposeful and productive participation in the environment, such as composting, can bring unexpected personal benefits as well as universal hope for fertile futures. We are not separate from our surroundings; we are part of them. Somehow humans seem to feel that their intellectual developments trump natural instincts and therefore separate us from the lower life forms. It may make us uniquely skilled, but we are never separate from the world around us and beneath our feet. We are one of its inhabitants, just one. Our choices and actions need to reflect a deep appreciation and understanding of the interconnectedness of all beings. We have a role among many in the grand scheme of things. Composting can enhance our experience within our environment.

Taking on the art of composting and the activities associated with composting, such as getting our hands in the dirt and growing fresh vegetables at home, undeniably opens new perspectives. We remember the natural world of our childhood. We learn to step back and slow down before acting. From this vantage point we can begin to see our choices more clearly as well as their effect on the creatures we share this world with. I can't  tell you how many times I have been distracted and found myself with my hand in the garbage can discarding a perfectly beautiful apple core! When I wake up from my distraction, I realize that I am denying the worms a fragrant, healthy meal. I inevitably reach into the wastebasket and retrieve it (luckily worms don't mind a bit of dust on their dinner). With pride, I bury it in my worm bin. It feels good to snap out of a state of distraction and engage directly with everyday life and the choices directly in front of me. It feels good to feed my worms and remember how hard they are working to take care of my waste. It is through living in the moment that individuals can make profound changes. When you are aware of your behavior and its consequences, you have the opportunity to act mindfully!

You may also end up with the best vegetable or flower garden on the block as well as a crew of new wriggly red worms to keep you company! Once you begin to reap the rich and aromatic benefits of composting, you will never go back. It is impossible not to take pride in the production of this beautiful and nutrient rich substance. You become part of the cycle of life in a very real and fruitful way.

THE FLOW OF YOUR LIFE

As with any new activity that you want to incorporate into your life, you must make sure that it fits. As you take on the discipline of composting, you need to find its place in the flow of your daily activities. There are ways to make this new activity fit right in. It is common practice when composting, no matter the type, to collect your kitchen scraps before adding them to your bin or pile of choice. This can streamline your efforts and reduce the number of trips you make from your kitchen to your site. In the case of worm composting, it is also often nice to collect a couple of days' worth of waste before distributing a new batch of food to the worms. I always say that like you and I, the worms don't like to be disturbed in the middle of their meal. Because much of our organic waste is produced in the kitchen while preparing meals, it is helpful to have a plan for storing your scraps that conveniently fits in your kitchen. Possibilities include:

1. Countertop receptacle: There are very nice ceramic, stainless steel, and bamboo countertop compost collectors available on the market today. Many of these, in addition to being attractive, have charcoal filter inserts that help to absorb odors that may arise from waste stored at room temperature. These are not meant to become your composter, just storage until you deliver it to your bin or pile. Compostable bag inserts, used in conjunction, will minimize the cleaning and ease of emptying as well.

2. Plastic container: An inexpensive plastic storage container sized to fit in your refrigerator is an economical and simple way to store and collect scraps. Just take it out when preparing food and replace with the lid intact in the refrigerator to keep scraps from spoiling and creating odors. Because this device does not have a built-in filter, storing it in the refrigerator is important to prevent odors.

3. Bin on site: With many methods of indoor composting, such as vermiculture or Bokashi buckets, it is possible to keep your bin local and dump your scraps directly into it. My worm bin is placed conveniently at the end of my counter. After collecting my scraps on the cutting board, I just remove the lid and bury them for the worms to eat. The same can be true when using the Bokashi bucket system. The closer it is, the more likely you are to use it!

DIY Compost Collection

Collecting food scraps is the initial step on the path to composting. If you don't want to purchase a new countertop compost collector, use something you already have in the house. Many everyday household items will work just fine and can become part of the finished product as well. Here are a few simple collection ideas:

Paper grocery bags: Not only do these work well to hold your groceries, they contain your kitchen scraps well, too. Simply add a sheet or two of newspaper or paper towels to the bottom of the bag to collect moisture and start adding your coffee grounds, peelings, and cores. Keep the top of the bag rolled down to prevent fruit flies from invading when not in use. Once this is full, dump the contents into your compost bin or pile. The paper bag is also compostable when added to a large bin or tumbler. If using a worm bin, make sure to tear the bag up into leaf-size pieces to ensure that the worms can break it and its contents down faster.

Newspaper: Though most of your newspaper may go to the recycling bin, repurpose a few sheets as a wrapper for your kitchen scrap collection. Like wrapping up a large burrito, add kitchen scraps to the center of the paper and wrap up. The newspaper, like the paper bag, can also be composted, adding a carbon source to the mix.

Milk cartons: An empty milk carton opens up easily to accept kitchen scraps and hold moisture in through its waxed lining. This makes a simple countertop collection device. A waxed milk carton is compostable in a high-temperature outdoor bin or tumbler as well but should not be fed to the worms. It will not break down easily within a slow, low-temperature compost bin, either.

Whether cleaning out your refrigerator or preparing a meal, your composting bin should be handy for disposing of your scraps. Many find indoor methods the simplest way to compost, especially in colder months when transporting your waste means putting on your boots and coat. We will go over various indoor methods in chapter six so you know your options. Remember, though composting may be new and require behavioral changes, it is essential for it to fit into your lifestyle or you will become frustrated and give up. Many a composting effort has failed due to impractical expectations—similar to dieting!

You might assume that composting is a skill learned and practiced by gardeners and those with a green thumb alone. This was a common mistake that I made as well. I wasn't a gardener when I started composting. Much of the reason that I came to this conclusion was because literature often pairs the two exclusively. I would like to change this false belief. I'm not arguing that the benefits of composting are not closely linked to the goals of gardeners, just the opposite. It is essential to start feeding our garden soil so that our food supply and earth's soil can continue to feed and nourish us with its produce and gorgeous blooms. But the truth is com-

posting can be embraced by all! City dwellers, including apartment and condo owners can compost for the larger good. The reduction of waste flow to our landfills is monumental. This modification in our behavior can actually begin to reverse the effects that our consumer-driven lives have on our planet's natural resources.

STEPS TO START

1. Think of yourself as a composter: Know you are able.
2. Become familiar with your habits: Do you spend much time in the kitchen? In the outdoors? Do you eat out more frequently than cook? (Eating out often, and having leftovers, may fit with a home Bokashi system where you don't need to monitor the type of food you are discarding—it takes everything: Meat, dairy, oils and spices galore!)
3. Get up-close and personal with your garbage: What do you discard? Yard waste? Veggie scraps? Garden waste? Paper products? Meat? How much are you throwing away each day? Per week? Watch and see how many garbage bags you are taking to the curb or alley. Notice how often you take out the garbage before it's full because it's a bit stinky from the organic waste materials beginning to break down. Once you sort and separate your trash for composting, you will eliminate the stinky garbage can under the sink or in the pantry.
4. Start to collect: Begin to collect your kitchen scraps in a receptacle on the kitchen counter. Train yourself to separate as you go. Dump the coffee grounds in first thing in the morning, drop the carrot peelings right in, scrape the leftover stems and tops off the cutting board right into the receptacle for later use.
5. Chose your method: Indoor or outdoor? Bin or pile, worms or Bokashi enzymes? Sheet/lasagna composting or trench composting? Read about each method in the following chapters to determine which will work best within your lifestyle and your home. What do you have time to maintain? How dirty are you willing to get? How patient are you? What is your goal? Compost for the garden or to minimize your garbage and waste stream? Both?

Don't forget that many individuals choose to have complementary systems. For example, a worm bin for kitchen scraps and an outdoor pile for yard waste.

6. Time to make the compost: Add your collected scraps to your chosen method. Depending on what method you chose, within weeks or months you will have your product: compost, black gold, compost tea, or liquid gold tea from Bokashi!

Now that you see yourself as a composter with some scraps waiting in the kitchen, the groundwork has been laid to begin. It may be helpful to take inventory of a couple things prior to running out and buying an expensive tumbler or a fancy electric indoor compost device.

Questions that may be helpful to answer:

1. Do you have a yard with space to manage a pile or a larger apparatus such as a tumbler?
2. Do you have a garden, shrubs, or trees that can benefit from your compost and/or worm castings? If not, have you talked with neighbors or friends who may be interested in using your finished compost?
3. Do you live in the city where rodents may be attracted to outdoor compost piles/bins?
4. Do you live in the mountains where bears and larger animals will be attracted by the smells of food?
5. Do you live in a climate where your pile or bin will freeze over in the cooler months?
6. Do you live in a dry climate? Is there an easy water source near by? Will you have the ability to keep a compost pile moist?
7. Are you looking to get a product out of your composting efforts in the near future (this season) or are you willing to wait a season or more to reap the benefits of your efforts?
8. Do you have any physical limitations that may limit your abilities to manage a larger

project like a heap or tumbler? If so, do you have support to assist you with the manual labor often required for these methods?

9. Lastly, can you already see how becoming a composter changes everything? Keep those eyes open and watch the world take on a new life.

After reviewing these basic guidelines and questions, you are ready to review the process actually taking place in a compost pile and be formally introduced to the team players. Though there is a method of composting that fits most lifestyles, a successful composting lifestyle requires a bit of conscious effort. Taking a little more time to understand the mechanisms at work will help to ensure a successful outcome.

4: Beneficial Bacteria and Fungal Friends

"I have always looked upon decay as being just as wonderful and rich an expression of life as growth."

—Henry Miller

Embarking on any method of composting is a team approach. If we think that the art of composting and its beautiful (and miraculous, in my opinion) rewards are solely a product of our own actions, we are mistaken. We choose to start collecting our waste and putting it to good use by adding it to a compost bin, but it is the magic of microbes, the wisdom of worms, and the skills of bacteria and fungus that transform our trash into nutrient-rich humus for the soil.

Without these amazing and often underappreciated creatures, our efforts would be for naught, and we would all be swimming in a sea of garbage. Even without our help, these organisms are constantly cleaning up after us, as they work their way through the Earth's surface debris and piles of waste we leave behind.

When we join forces with these small creatures, working alongside them in a compost or worm bin, we are consistently reminded of our interconnections to the other living beings on the planet. An awareness of the compost workforce can remind us to step back a little, gain a new perspective, slow down, and let some natural intelligence lead us to balance.

Compost thrives in the presence of various microscopic bacteria, fungi, nematodes, tiny mites, springtails, and spiders, in addition to the wriggly worms, centipedes, and slugs that are more easily visible. Yes it's true, all of these creatures become our neighbors, living and working beside us in our composting efforts. We make friends with nature's creatures and get to know their skills and preferences. The beauty of engaging in the activity of composting is that it is a collaborative process made richer by the diversity of the organisms that assist us. The more diverse the ecosystem, the more efficiently the waste is transformed. The more diverse the organic material, the richer, more nutritious, and balanced the compost produced.

When I counsel people about the basics of a nutritious diet, I always refer to the colors and varieties of vegetables as an essential and simple way of consuming a balanced diet. Color is not just a tool for the artist's pallet; it is a source of inspiration for each of us. Make a beautiful salad and it is almost guaranteed to be nutritious! Increase the value of your pasta by adding a colored vegetable. There is a similar consideration with composting. "Browns" and "greens" are terms to classify carbon- and nitrogen-rich waste. (These terms are used not to specify the visual color but to describe the amount of carbon or nitrogen a particular item contains.) As in the diet, diversity adds nutrients to your compost. Different species of microorganisms prefer different hosts and thrive in different conditions. Be colorful with your diet and your compost will be headed in the right direction. You and your compost will be packed rich with nutrients!

THE CLEANER, THE FASTER, THE BETTER?

Developments in sanitation, hygiene, and technology often steer us away from the natural world, promising ease and cleanliness in all areas of our lives. We therefore lose sight of the tiny, yet highly skilled members of the ecosystem. We may even come to avoid or fear bacteria and microscopic intruders in our homes and bodies. Our antibacterial soaps and most cleaning products target these creatures as if they were our enemies. These microscopic creatures have critical roles in disease and illness. Drugs such as antibiotics target and eliminate pathogens allowing us to live longer. But we may be missing something in our efforts to live longer, faster, and cleaner lives. Our advances must not blind us to the natural cycles and rhythms of the earth. If we eradicate nature's creatures purposefully or accidentally, we will suffer the consequences of going it alone. For example, the digestive system is home to trillions of microbes and bacteria that perform important roles such as eliminating harmful germs, aiding digestion, and protecting the lining of your intestinal tract, all of which contribute to a highly functioning immune system. In fact, some of your favorite foods may contain microbes, such as yogurt, sauerkraut, buttermilk, kefir, and miso soup. Nutritionists claim that eating foods with good bacteria helps reduce harmful bacteria that contribute to problems such as diarrhea, yeast infections, colds and flu, eczema, and irritable bowel syndrome.[1]

Though we need to preserve our own health and be aware of pathogenic and harmful bacteria, lets not ignore the friendly fungi along the way. In fact, the antibiotic penicillin actually was developed from a fungus! Similarly in nature, specialized fungi that exist in a balanced compost pile produce natural antibiotics that keep plant disease at bay when later applied to the garden. This is yet another example of the need to nurture diversity for natural health. Composting requires participation of microorganisms and insects and therefore requires us to rethink many of the fears and limited views we hold about cleanliness and bugs.

In short, killing off all bugs and bacteria—beneficial along with the harmful—is not the quick fix we need. The *Chicago Tribune* reported on a

1. Elizabeth Smoots, "Healthy Bacteria Aids Digestion, Fights Disease," HeraldNet, www.heraldnet.com/article/20080129/LIVING/861706168 (accessed April 6, 2010).

new study regarding dirt and children's health. Initial research showed that people exposed to and occasionally ingesting dirt as young children may be at less risk for some adult cardiac problems. The microorganisms in the dirt may actually protect the body and build the immune system for better disease fighting![2] How incredible is that! We shouldn't eliminate or reject our advances in health but it wouldn't hurt to maintain a broader perspective: Cleaner may not always be better.

DIVERSITY YIELDS STRENGTH

Nature's diversity is its strength. In a healthy compost pile, all of the organisms work until their job is finished. Then they die off to become food for the next phase of decomposition led by another team member. When this cycle of life and death is kept in balance, the creatures thrive and work in tandem to keep the larger process moving. The release and reuse of nature's elements occurs as nutrients and minerals are cycled back to create more life. The creatures store nutrients, such as nitrogen, in their bodies, which prevents the loss of this valuable life-giving substance.

People exposed to and occasionally ingesting dirt as young children may be at less risk for some adult cardiac problems.

When they die, other organisms feed on the stored nutrients in the bodies, ensuring the nutrients aren't lost. This is another reason why creating your own nutrient-rich soil is better for the environment. Chemical fertilizers, in addition to adding toxins, are not as stable in the soil and are therefore lost at high rates through washout and leaching.

The benefits of building relationships with Earth's tiny and sometimes slimy creatures do not stop in the soil or the garden. They extend into our lives in many unexpected ways. They can teach us gratitude and compassion as we learn to nurture their communities and reap the benefits of their hard work. This awareness reminds us that humans exist with, not apart from, our environment. Ancient civilizations lived according to the cycles of the moon, sun, oceans, and life and death. They prioritized feeding the

2. Robert Channick, "NU Study: Dirt's Good for Kids," *Chicago Tribune*, March 24, 2010, www.chicagotribune.com/health/ct-x-n-health-dirt-20100324,0,6756958.story, (accessed March 31, 2010).

soil and thanking the animals whose lives were taken for food, clothing, and shelters. If we slow down, take a closer look, learn to listen and get a little dirty when composting, then we will inevitably enhance our experience of the world around us while sharing it with amazing and essential creatures. Many new worm keepers express excitement about housing their thousand new friends. At the same time, they verbalize a worry that they will harm their new friends. This type of compassion and caring attitude makes a great worm guardian and a great friend and neighbor.

LET THE FEAST BEGIN

As soon as a pile of waste such as yard or kitchen scraps appears, the frenzied work of various organisms starts. At each phase of decomposition, a different worker dominates. Whether you are hosting a worm bin, a hot or cold compost pile, or a Bokashi bucket, various organisms show up. It's true that your work is the least important, yet it's completely

Slow down, take a closer look, learn to listen, and get a little dirty.

essential in the composting process. Becoming aware of the needs of the critters in your compost enables you to properly care for them and help them to thrive. This in turn keeps the cycles of life and death moving, taking your kitchen scraps through the process of decay and returning them to the earth where they came from.

Creating the right environment for your compost and its critters is key. Similar to our own survival needs, there are four essential elements in the survival of these creatures: temperature, moisture, oxygen, and energy or food. Different creatures require different combinations or levels of these essential elements to survive and thrive. Obviously, their home environment is a key component as evidenced by the fact that the anaerobic state of a landfill is not conducive to efficient bacterial and fungal activity needed for typical composting decomposition. Composting will actually be much less work for you if you utilize the workforce on hand to do the job of transforming garbage and waste into humus-rich soil.

Though there are many methods to create compost at home, most individuals use the decomposition model. There are many creatures that need to be present to help decomposition. How decomposition occurs also varies. Some bacteria do thrive in anaerobic (without oxygen) environments and others in aerobic-rich environments. A traditional compost pit or bin functions within an aerobic, oxygen-rich environment. Bokashi buckets, on the other hand, rely on a specific type of anaerobic (oxygen free) environment. Unlike a landfill, the anaerobic environment of a Bokashi bucket is monitored to encourage fermentation of the waste. Specialized enzymes are added to the waste to assist in fermentation and encourage anaerobic bacteria to thrive. This method is one of the few anaerobic forms of composting and will be described further in later chapters.

In contrast, a worm bin is a form of consumption versus decomposition. The worms actually eat your garbage! Full decay should not occur. The worms consume your kitchen scraps before decomposition has a chance to occur, although the outcome is similar to that of decomposition: rich castings composed of nutrients, minerals and humus. Like humans, worms rely on the microbial and bacterial activity to make the food they ingest easier to digest. As you may expect, worms also need to recruit bacteria and fungi to breakdown their meals. In a worm bin, a diverse ecosystem is still required. The point is, to be successful with your composting efforts, it is important to have an awareness of the needs of the workers to make them happy and productive.

AEROBIC DECOMPOSITION ESSENTIALS

When embarking on a composting adventure, most individuals are introduced to outdoor compost bins and heaps. I find it helpful to first understand this traditional method before contrasting other processes, such as a worm bin or the Bokashi method. Because this process of organic waste reuse relies on decomposition, it requires an oxygen-rich environment to thrive. (It is possible for decomposition to take place anaerobically but this is not what we strive for in a compost pile or bin.) A sure sign of anaerobic decomposition is the stink that many equate with a compost pile or heap. A foul, decaying odor is usually a sign that there is a problem; your compost lacks oxygen! Your senses, including smell, along with basic assessment skills and checklists will help guide you in your efforts and ensure success. In addition to oxygen, the bacteria and fungi that initiate the process of breaking down organic matter require moisture and varied temperatures to best do their work.

There are hundreds of kinds of bacteria that show up in a compost pile. It is impossible for the average person to keep track of them all, but there are three main types that you should be familiar with so you can best support their efforts: *psychrophiles, mesophiles,* and *thermophiles.* These three types of bacteria are categorized based on their temperature preference. Certain bacteria prefer hot, humid environments and others prefer cool, airy climates. In this case, climate refers to the conditions inside the compost pile, not the environment the pile is placed in.

Bacteria that show up early in the scene, psychrophiles, are not too concerned with the actual makeup of the waste. These low-temperature bacteria initiate a process of decomposition. Whether it's a cold or hot compost pile, they are present. Before the heat begins, these members of the team arrive at the scene and begin to release amino acids from the waste. Though they can still functionally assist breakdown at temperatures as low as 28° F (-2° C), they prefer temperatures around 55° F (13° C). As decomposition continues and the microbes oxidize the carbon compounds, heat is generated. This heat, along with a warm ambient temperature, encourages the next phase of troops to arrive.

The mesophiles arrive when the pile heats up to approximately 68° F (20° C), and they can survive in temperatures as high as 86° F (30° C). They are very efficient decomposers and are responsible for most of the activity that occurs in a compost pile, whether it is hot or cold.

High-temperature bacteria are called thermophiles and these are bacteria that make your compost hot. They can survive temperatures as high as 160° F (71° C), doing their best work along the way. An egg could be boiled in the center of a hot compost pile when these thermophiles are abundant. Quite amazing!

HOW THE PILE HEATS UP

The outside temperature will affect the internal temperature of your compost pile or bin but it is not solely responsible for it. Fitting in with the intelligence seen throughout nature, certain types of bacteria create the heat needed to support other types of bacteria. Heat is generated as the bacteria ingest carbon for energy through a process known as oxidization. Bacteria are rapidly burning up the carbon and heating up the pile. You may have heard of the carbon:nitrogen ratio needed to maintain a compost pile; carbon provides energy for the bacteria to do their work, and the nitrogen encourages bacteria to grow and reproduce. The ratio is also essential for heating up the compost pile, which encourages new bacteria populations.

If the right conditions are in place to support the bacteria, the temperatures will continue to rise. Bacteria need the right combination of energy and nutrients (carbon and nitrogen) as well as plenty of oxygen and moisture for this to occur. The proper carbon:nitrogen ratio of 30:1 is the guideline followed by many composters. There are many different ways to achieve this ratio but the basic idea is to mix carbon-based "browns" and nitrogen-based "greens" equally. We will further explore the carbon:nitrogen ratio on page 59.

The presence of water and air is an important part of the process. Turning a pile ensures air circulation and will give you a feel for the moisture content of your composting matter. Compost should have a moisture content between 40 and 60 percent, similar in feel to a well wrung out sponge. When monitored with these things in mind, the temperature of the pile will rise. As temperatures

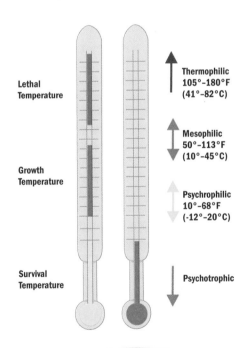

Three specific bacteria groups thrive within compost based on the internal temperature of the bin or pile.

Lethal Temperature

Growth Temperature

Survival Temperature

Thermophilic
105°–180°F
(41°–82°C)

Mesophilic
50°–113°F
(10°–45°C)

Psychrophilic
10°–68°F
(-12°–20°C)

Psychotrophic

rise, thermophiles take over. This essential part of the process turns a cold compost into a hot compost. It is not essential for all compost to reach the high temperatures supporting theromophilic activity. But, this hot compost method speeds up the process of decomposition and, in addition, kills off pathogens and weed seeds in the compost material. When temperatures of 100° F to 160° F (38° C to 71° C) are maintained for three to five days, the heat will kill any remaining pathogens as well as any weed seeds contained in the pile.

Cold compost, led by mesophiles and psychrophiles, either never reaches the high temperature or doesn't sustain it for the three to five days necessary to kill the weed seeds and pathogens. Though both situations will eventually yield gorgeous products full of nutrients for the soil, a cold compost can take as long as a year to do what a hot compost can do in two to three weeks time! This comes as a shock and may be a bit of a disappointment for many novice composters, but it's important to consider when choosing the method of composting that works best for you. In addition, added efforts may be needed to prevent weed seeds from moving into your garden when adding cold compost. This cold compost can contains weed seeds that may take a free ride into the garden and flourish within the fertile compost soil.

Temperatures may continue to shift over time depending on the conditions supporting your bacteria populations. If monitored, a hot compost can be encouraged to heat up two or three times even after it has cooled down. Throughout the entire process, low- and mid-temperature fungi are also breaking down the cellulose and lignin found in woodier materials. Mid-temperature fungi called *actinomycetes* and *streptomycetes* perform very specialized skills in compost. They are responsible for creating natural plant antibiotics and are always welcome additions to a healthy compost pile. The enzymes and organic nutrients they pass on to plants is shown to decrease disease and build plant vitality. At times, you may see them working their way through your compost as thin, white, cobweb-like structures. These webs of grayish-white fungus should not be confused with green molds that may smell strong and unpleasant and be a sign of poor oxygen flow in a compost. These little, whitish webs of life are responsible for the rich, earthy smell of happy compost!

Ants, Fungus, and Biofuels

Leaf cutter ants in South America actually farm a specific type of fungus within their colonies. These creative and resourceful ants skillfully slice and carry large pieces of leaves across the jungle accumulating an incredible surplus. The leaves are not used as sustenance for survival as one might suspect; instead the

ants intentionally use the fragments of leaves to grow fungus, similar to the way we rely on fungus and bacteria to grow within our compost pile. The ants then ingest this fungus for their sustenance. Our gardens reap the benefits of compost created by the fungi in our piles. Just as the ants feed the fungus leaves, we feed the fungus and bacteria in our compost piles scraps of waste to help them produce fertile soil. The process of decomposition in both the leaf piles and compost piles attracts the fungus and then subsequently feeds it and helps it flourish. This is an incredible example of the value of fungus in the natural world as well as the wisdom of the natural way.

Scientists are also studying the enzymes these ants secrete for cutting and slicing the leaves. The efficiency with which these ants break down the plant cell walls may be the key to the industrial process needed to make biofuels. This is another example of biomimicry in action. Scientists are watching and learning from nature in their quest for new technologies. We should be doing the same.

THE CARBON:NITROGEN STORY

After a great deal of research and practical experience, I have to admit that I still struggle to simplify the concepts around carbon and nitrogen in relation to composting. As mentioned, a carbon:nitrogen (C:N) ratio of 30:1 is recommended. A combination of carbon-rich materials mixed with nitrogen-rich materials is essential for a traditional compost pile to transform waste into a nutrient-rich product for the garden. It is not a rigid measurement but a guideline pointing to the importance of both materials and their dominance in the mix. Cooking seems to be the best example to help achieve a better understanding of the C:N ratio. Recipes are important, yet once we have a general understanding of our ingredients, we can use a bit of creativity in the mix. The same is true in compost.

Butter, sugar, flour, and eggs combine to make delicious cookie dough. Alone, those ingredients are not cookie dough. The measure of each ingredient in relation to the others will help create the texture and taste needed to satisfy our sweet cravings. Once the essential ingredients are in the mix, we may vary the recipe to meet our needs. Similarly, carbon-based materials and nitrogen-based materials complement each other when combined properly to make the best crumbling black compost.

When cooking, recipes often encourage adding an additional tablespoon of salt, some chocolate chips, or a drizzle of oil to enhance the taste or texture of a dish. In composting, it is essential to start with a combination of materials, and specifically adding a bit more carbon or nitrogen may affect the texture, nutritional composition, and "cooking time" of your compost. The product is improved by sticking close to the guidelines, yet there is room for variability.

But what does this really mean? How do you achieve this ratio? What happens if you don't? The carbon:nitrogen story starts with the description of organic materials as "browns" and "greens." This description may be familiar to many and still not fully understood. A better understanding of each material's composition will lead to more successful composting.

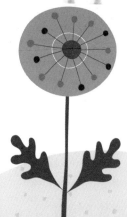

Once the reasoning behind the ratio is revealed, the magic of the ingredients and their combined effects will be clear. Clarifying this will be helpful and may take the frustration out of the compost equation. You will feel more confident to add a dash of green or a handful of brown to improve your product.

The colors, brown and green, are in reference to the basic dominance of carbon versus nitrogen in the organic materials you are composting. Brown materials refer to the drier, carbon-rich materials. These browns tend to be dead and dry and brown in color, such as leaves, straw, and wood chips. Plant cellulose is a carbon-based material, so plant by-products, such as hay, straw, weeds, and even paper products (if ground to the proper consistency) will provide the necessary carbon. Though essential, carbon-based materials decompose slowly and need some assistance. Enter the green materials.

Greens tend to be alive, wet, and often green in color, such as fresh grass clippings and food waste. Fresh, wet materials, which are higher in nitrogen, decompose faster than older, drier, and woodier tissues that are high in carbon. The addition of these green materials is essential to give those older, drier organics a bit of a kick-start. Also, like humans, microorganisms need a balanced diet. The mix is truly the key to the composting riddle. Keep those microorganisms happy and healthy and you don't have to worry about much more.

As mentioned, the ideal C:N ratio is 25:1 or 30:1 depending on whom you consult. This ratio describes the chemical composition of a material. It does not mean that you need a volume of brown materials that is thirty-times greater than the volume of green matter. The C:N ratio of a combined pile of compost is a complex calculation based on each individual materials chemical composition. For example, the C:N ratio of wood chips is 700:1 while the C:N ratio of fresh grass clippings is 17:1. When added to a compost at the same time, the wood chips and grass clippings will help the microorganisms to stay fed, active, and in balance, and, therefore, heat up appropriately. The amount of activity (heat) will also depend on the volume of each material added. Some recommend adding a volume measurement of half carbon to half nitrogen, others follow a guideline of two-thirds addition of carbon to one-third nitrogen as a rule of thumb.

As a novice, it may be helpful to keep in mind that diversity of ingredients is important to ensure a balanced compost and a sufficient C:N ratio. If you have an abundance of grass clippings (high nitrogen), the compost may be heating up but become quite slimy and eventually limit oxygen flow. This is a bit like runny cookie dough that lacks the proper amount of flour to bind it together. The lack of oxygen will eventually create a putrid odor and shift the environment towards an anaerobic one, not so conducive to composting. On the other hand, too many dried leaves (carbon) may compress and mat down with little or no activity due to the lack of nitrogen needed to get the leaves cooking. Just remember, the more diversified the mix, the more microorganisms go to work.

Why the Carbon:Nitrogen Ratio Is Important

A balanced diet for the microorganisms that digest compost is about 30 parts carbon for every one part of nitrogen that they consume. Therefore, for a hot pile with temperatures up to 140° F (60° C), the C:N ratio of all the materials should average 30:1. At that ratio, you can rest assured that the microbes are stuffing themselves. Of course, this is ideal; your pile may not necessarily obtain this ratio. A ratio of 50:1 is adequate for most slower, and therefore lower-temperature, piles. A pile with a ratio between 25:1 and 50:1 will breakdown steadily and yield nutrient-rich compost, although the closer you get to a 25:1 ratio, the hotter your pile is going to be and therefore the more consistently productive.

If we go a little deeper into the importance of maintaining the proper ratio, we find that if there's too much nitrogen in your pile, this plant-loving element will be expelled from your pile and essentially wasted. At a C:N ratio of 30:1, only one-half of 1 percent of nitrogen will be lost. However, if there is excess nitrogen, over 60 percent will escape into the atmosphere. For the serious composter or gardener, these facts make a big difference. The loss of nitrogen is a real shame when taking into account the important role that nitrogen plays in plant growth. Additionally, excess nitrogen causes an increase in the pH level creating an acidic environment. The acidic environment can be toxic for some microorganisms and, therefore, will also decrease the diversity of soil life you will be adding back to the garden and supporting in your compost.

A C:N ratio of 25:1 or 30:1 promotes rapid composting and allows for some leftover nitrogen in the finished compost. This nitrogen-rich end product of compost promotes vigorous plant growth. You can be confident when you use it in the garden you are nourishing the life there.

As you master the skill of creating your carbon to nitrogen mix, you often have another obstacle. One of the most challenging aspects for those who begin composting is to gather the right mix of materials at the right time to support this perfect C:N ratio. After mowing the lawn, you may have an abundance of nitrogen-based materials. In contrast, after raking the dry fall leaves, you will be stocked with carbon-based browns. Because it is often difficult to maintain the perfect mix of materials on hand to support the recommended 25:1 or 30:1 ratio, it is important to know that you can still successfully compost all organic matter. To be composted, materials really only need to be biodegradable and have nutrients usable by the compost microorganisms on hand.

If the proper C:N ratio is kept in mind by consistently adding a mix of both greens and browns consistently, the compost can thrive and deliver a rich, earthy product. In addition, you may avoid extreme odors and nutrient loss along the way by sticking close to the guidelines the ratio provides, but don't let this complex equation keep you from composting. As with cooking, you can follow a recipe or you can add a dash of this and a little sprinkle of that until you get just the right mix of ingredients to meet your needs. Be a little creative and keep the end result in mind.

Carbon:Nitrogen Ratio
for Common Compost Material

GREEN	BROWN
Aged chicken manure, 7:1	Woody chips and twigs, 700:1
Humus, 10:1	Sawdust, 500:1
Fresh grass clippings, 17:1	Shredded newspaper, 175:1
Fresh weeds, 20:1	Straw, hay, 90:1
Rotten manure, 20:1	Pine needles, 80:1
Vegetable scraps, 25:1	Leaves, 60–80:1
Coffee grounds, 25:1	Corn stalks, 60:1
Fruit wastes, 25–40:1	Peat moss, 58:1
Garden waste, 30:1	Nut shells, 35:1

THE CREATURES YOU SEE IN YOUR COMPOST

As you familiarize yourself with the look, feel, smell, and temperature of your compost efforts, you will probably see lots of wriggling and scurrying going on. Like the webs of fungi, these added signs of life confirm the presence of additional team members. Small mites, springtails, pot worms, and earthworms all help to further break down the organic waste in most composting methods. The exception to this is within an anaerobic process of composting, such as Bokashi or the in-home electric composter, the NatureMill. Don't expect an added workforce of small insects or bugs in Bokashi buckets or the NatureMill; their processes are completed without the additional assistance of insects and worms. But don't be fooled, even the bacteria are hard at work within both of these composting methods.

It may be difficult for many beginning composters to accept the presence of these insects so close to our homes, hands, and gardens. Yet these insects are as important in maintaining a healthy compost ecosystem as the soil bacteria and fungi we have come to understand and therefore appreciate. But, you do not need to allow certain creatures to proliferate and become a nuisance. The most common complaints that discourage individuals are the presence or infestation of maggots and fruit flies.

Maggots are a stage of fly larvae and may need to be controlled (see sidebar on controlling flies). Be aware, though, that there are several types of maggots and some that may even be expert compost assistants. Common housefly larvae are not beneficial and are known to carry as many as sixty-five different diseases. They will thrive in the compost environments and make a nuisance of themselves. In contrast, the larvae of the black soldier fly is a friend in your bin. Though they may proliferate and become numerous, soldier flies do not bite and are not known to transmit any diseases. In addition, their presence minimizes the breeding potential for houseflies. The black soldier fly larvae is your ally in composting as well as in housefly control. They are voracious composters of decaying material.

Fruit flies also thrive on exposed food and organic materials. The compost pile or bin can be a paradise for them. They are not harmful but are clearly distracting and annoying when we open the lid of our bin to add new food scraps. We may even be adding fruit fly larvae to our compost as we deposit fruit skins and peels. To minimize their presence,

Controlling Flies

Indian composting experts claim that colonies of flies can be kept under control with 3 tablespoons of red chili powder and a good stirring up each week. If this does not work for your pile, try covering your compost with a fine screening or capping the compost with a piece of sod. This may deter the

parent flies from landing on top of the contents to deposit their eggs. Though some flies may be a benefit to the compost pile, keeping their population under control may help you to enjoy your composting experience more.

cover all new food scrap additions with a handful of dry materials, such as leaves, sawdust, or shredded newspaper. If you are composting in an exposed heap, place a tarp or an old carpet remnant over top to deter parents from laying eggs. Fruit fly traps will be discussed further in chapters 7 and 8. Once an infestation occurs, it may be necessary to take the time to treat the situation at hand. Too many composting stories end with disgust over the state of a fly-infested bin when measures could be taken to minimize the annoyance and control the reoccurrence.

Frustrations with pests should not be the endnote in your composting efforts. Though flies are often present for periods of time, you can minimize their populations and learn to work with their cycles while continuing along on your dedicated path of environmental stewardship.

5: Composting Outdoors

"Once we no longer live beneath our mother's hearth, it is the earth with which we form the same dependent relationship, relying ... on its cycles and elements, helpless without its protective embrace."

—Louise Erdrich

A plot of land can be used for many things. There is nothing like lazing around the yard on a summer day, tossing the Frisbee with friends, playing with pets, tending a garden, growing edibles and, don't forget, composting. Having outdoor space opens up a world of opportunities for various methods of composting on site. Heaps, tumblers, bins, trenches, and digesters work great in outdoor spaces.

One of the joys of producing compost is that we have most of the elements necessary to start right in our homes. Our waste stream creates the bulk of organic materials necessary to begin the process of decomposition needed for composting. Most of these organics can be recycled through building a compost on site, right in our own backyards.

Today many municipalities are planning large-scale organic waste removal. A couple have built composting facilities to manage this waste stream more effectively. Curbside pick up of separated organic waste is slowly becoming a reality across the country. Multiple color-coded bins line the streets of many neighborhoods in Seattle, Portland, and San Francisco. Organic waste, recyclables, and the remaining trash is separated by bin prior to pick up. The City of San Francisco had a particularly progressive goal to divert 75 percent of waste generated in the city away from landfill disposal by the end of 2010 and to achieve zero waste by 2020. It is actually illegal to throw away your banana peels and coffee grounds in San Francisco. Imagine that.

I am in favor of these municipal programs that support organic waste removal and mass composting. But, imagine if we all contributed locally, right on our own property. As it stands, many cities do not currently have the finances or infrastructure to implement these large-scale projects.

Yard waste makes up two-thirds of the waste stream.

With individual compost efforts we could help eliminate much of the energy required for the transport and processing of massive amounts of waste, reducing our carbon footprint and nourishing our local soils along the way. In addition to our kitchen scraps, we can utilize our yard waste, grass clippings, leaves, spent garden stalks, twigs, and weeds to bulk up and heat up our compost bin, pile, or heap. At the same time, we would greatly reduce our landfill contributions because yard waste makes up two-thirds of the waste stream.

Composting is not limited to the outdoors, but most people associate composting with outside methods. There are many different ways to begin your composting efforts.

Even outdoor methods vary depending on your lifestyle. If outdoor composting seems right for you, its time to get a bin and start loading it up with your kitchen scraps, right? Sounds easy enough, and it can be, but there are some key factors you should consider to ensure that you choose the best outdoor method for your particular home and situation. Not all methods will be successful for all people.

The amount of information and products available can complicate the matter further. Local garden stores, retail suppliers, and online shopping venues are filled with compost supplies and apparatus. A growing awareness around waste reduction and the benefits of composting is flooding the market with new product designs that promise the best results in short periods of time. Many of these store-bought bins and tumblers promise fast transition from garbage to compost, simple retrieval of compost and pest-resistant designs. Be cautious and do your homework. It is best to learn a bit more before you make a final purchase. You may be disappointed with the outcome of your efforts if you don't invest a bit of time in the decision-making process. If bears are your local pests, "pest resistant" may have a whole new meaning. If you live in a cold climate, there is little chance of creating quick compost during the winter despite a promise of four-to-six weeks for your return.

The art of composting is in the mix—the mix of materials (your waste stream contents), know-how (understanding the process), and keeping the microorganisms recruited happy (bacteria and fungi). Even the best design may fail if you are missing one of these key ingredients. As you know from chapter 4, first and foremost you need to keep the "team" of bacteria and fungi happy, healthy, and hungry to be successful with composting. Keep this in mind when you are house hunting for your team and dedicating time and energy to sheltering your workforce. Not all homes are the same. It is not necessary to purchase the Cadillac of composters to be successful in your efforts, either. Many low-cost options work just as well as the best designed, high-cost tumbler.

As we explore various outdoor composting methods, you will see that there are two main considerations for your outdoor composting: how you will contain your materials for composting and what amount of space you can dedicate to this composting effort. Cost may also be a personal consideration for many and will be addressed as well. Fortunately, there are many low-cost strategies in the composting arena.

TO CONTAIN OR NOT TO CONTAIN?

The traditional compost pile was located far out, towards the back of a rural yard. The distance from the house was key in minimizing odors and possible pests, which would be disturbing closer to the house. It was usually a large heap of materials piled up over time and left to breakdown at its own pace. Many of my friends who grew up in the Midwest tell stories of trekking out to their particular pile under the heat of the summer sun with a bucket full of scraps as one of their household chores. The stories that follow usually involved sweating, various nasty odors, and an abundance of flies chasing them back to the house. It is not a surprise that many of them don't consider composting these days. The memories override their desire to reduce their waste stream. Though this type of heap is still frequently used to date, there are other options for suburban and urban folks whose neighbors may not appreciate the heap on their property line, for anyone who may not want to venture so far to deliver their scraps, and for those who want a cleaner-looking method.

The goal of containing your compost in a barrel, bin, tumbler, pit, or trench outdoors is multifaceted and includes: odor containment, pest deterrence, moisture and heat retention, convenience, and appearance. In order for your composting efforts to be successful, you will need to fit them into your lifestyle and home environment with the least amount of extra time and energy. A smooth transition is important. Down the road, when you have mastered the art of composting, you may choose to dedicate more time, energy, and space to your compost. It is easy to prioritize composting once you begin to reap the benefits and see the miraculous transformation of garbage into black gold!

Black gold is simply another widely used name for compost. It refers to the highly refined, nutrient-rich properties of finished compost. This inexpensive, homemade soil amendment is the key to healthy soil.

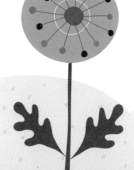

Odors & Pests

Obviously, garbage and kitchen waste may smell less than desirable as it begins to decompose, even aerobically. Food doesn't smell so hot when it starts to get old in the refrigerator, either. A closed system for composting, one with a lid or a natural dirt cover, such as in a trench, will contain odors more than an open pile or heap. If you do not have a large plot of land to specifically designate a zone for an open compost heap or pile, you may want to consider a closed system for this reason.

Outdoor space should be enjoyed, not avoided because of a strong smell from an open heap. Just because a closed system contains the odors doesn't mean that critters and local vermin may not still be curious and make frantic attempts to break in and steal your valuable scraps. This is their nature and they can't be blamed for trying to keep themselves and their critter families well fed. Many folks have seen a fat squirrel or mouse enter and exit their plastic barrels through a hole carefully chewed through the pest resistant plastic. Despite this possibility, the green or black recycled-plastic backyard compost container is widely and effectively used in suburban and urban homes today. In fact, many municipalities are subsidizing the purchase of these devices across the country to encourage reduction of organic waste. Be aware that many pests can still outsmart us and invade these bins. They will leave behind plenty of composting materials but the integrity of the bin will be compromised, and they may leave more of their own waste behind in the process of their thievery. The contents of their waste may contain toxins, bacteria, and materials that we did not plan to introduce to our gardens. This should be taken into consideration when growing edibles with your harvested compost. If you plan to use your composter primarily as a waste reduction method, then this may not be as much of a concern. If you are an avid gardener and want pure compost for your edible garden, take extra care to attain high temperatures. These high temperatures will kill any pathogens left behind by local critters. See the hot composting sidebar on page 72 for ideas.

There are several manufactured models with double-walled design that may want to consider if you are concerned about your neighborhood pests. The added barrier is much more effective at deterring squirrels, rats, and raccoons who may be easily able to chew through a single-walled design. However, the cost may be considerably more for these models. Shop around as new designs are entering the market every day. The scent of ammonia is also a great animal pest deterrent. Soak some strips of fabric and tie them to surrounding trees or fence poles. As the wind blows through the yard, the scent of ammonia marks the territory around the compost bin as undesirable, protecting your apparatus from attack.

Openings for ventilation and exposure to the ground below are a necessary feature of many bins and barrels. These small openings allow insects access to your bin and its contents. When local worms are able to crawl up from the ground below, they are able to begin stirring and aerating your compost. Their skills will speed up the transformation of your waste materials. Don't worry if other critters, including small beetles, sowbugs, pot worms, mites, and spiders, enter through these holes. These small critters contribute to the composting of the materials inside. Other flying or wiggly creatures, such as maggots and fruit flies may make their way in as well. They are less desirable due to their buzzing pesky nature. Make it a goal to minimize or control the populations of these pests early on by keeping food scraps fully covered.

Temperature

Another reason many people choose a contained composting system is in the hope that it will work harder within a contained and frequently hot atmosphere. Though this may be true on some level, it is a bit of a misconception. Cold outdoor temps certainly can cool down your compost pile, and that should be expected during winter months. Yet in reality, the outside temperature is not the main factor generating the heat needed for a hot compost, the microorganisms are. Remember those mid and high temperature bacteria colonies from

 Composting is easy, but even the experts get stumped about maintaining an active pile in extreme climates and during the change of seasons. It is important to understand that composting requires various components and no matter the temperature change, it can continue successfully, if the components are modified accordingly.

Hot Composting

All composting depends on bacteria. Outdoor composting, regardless of the apparatus or choice of containment, requires various temperature-specific bacteria to get the job done. To better understand the process, we can describe our efforts as "hot" or "cold" depending on the primary bacteria recruited, the time frame for transformation, and the composition of materials utilized. Not all compost piles, heaps, or bins achieve the high temperatures bacterial colonization required to be "hot."

There is a lot of buzz around the topic of hot composting (it reminds me of the recent surge of interest in "hot yoga" often called Bikram). Similar to the extra hot room required to make a Bikram hot yoga class beneficial to the human body, hot composting requires temperatures to rise inside the organic matter to fully benefit the transformation of matter. Within a Bikram yoga class, the heat allows individuals the benefit of more supple and flexible tissues. These supple, warm tissues lend themselves to increased flexibility, allowing the body to more easily perform the challenging poses. The average temperature in a Bikram yoga class is between 90° and 100° F (32° and 38° C).

A compost pile needs to heat up to at least 140° F (60° C) to qualify as "hot," and there are added benefits to heat in compost as well. In a hot compost, the thermophilic bacteria work hard to break down matter, transform waste, and release nutrients. At hot compost temperatures, they are also engaged in killing off enemies: pathogenic bacteria and weed seeds. Both are harmful to gardens and lawns. Pathogenic bacteria can spread disease among new seedlings or existing plants, and weed seeds can proliferate where your garden should be growing.

Both hot and cold composting transform our waste. The end products can look and feel very similar, yet the time to achieve transformation is significantly less in truly hot compost. This method requires a large bulk of materials, careful monitoring, and adequate space, but the transformation is fast. While a cold compost can take upwards of a year to complete, a hot compost can do the same job in mere weeks or months.

chapter 4—the thermophiles? These are the primary mechanisms for heat generation. Therefore, simply purchasing a closed container will not ensure that your compost achieves the proper heat for hot composting or that it retains heat during the winter. It will take specific efforts and constant attention to detail to ensure that an open or contained compost generates heat during freezing temperatures. This is a skill mastered by few. I encourage adding kitchen scraps to an outdoor unit year-round, but do not expect the microorganisms to be generating much heat for the cold months. They will be sitting dormant within the frozen food scraps, waiting for warmer days to get back to work. Don't worry, they will start right up once spring arrives.

In addition, if you live in an arid or hot, humid region of the world, contained air and heat can be a challenge. At this end of the temperature spectrum, special considerations will be required to minimize over-heating, drying of organic waste materials, and condensation levels contained under a lid. Sufficient ventilation and moisture levels will need to be understood and monitored to maximize temperature ranges. In this situation, a closed bin may heat up quickly and kill off many of the bacterial colonies required for steady decomposition. In addition to the extremes in temperature that can be achieved quickly in this type of closed environment, moisture can either be nonexistent or too abundant.

In an arid region, moisture may need to be added with each addition of waste and maintained through some creative covering methods (see the tips on the next page). Dried, petrified, organic waste does not decompose, it settles in for a long, dry stay at the bottom of your compost barrel.

In opposition to this, in a hot, humid environment, moisture can create significant condensation as it breaks down, causing the temperatures to rise even higher, potentially harming the bacteria. Condensation levels may rise dramatically if you are containing this moist waste within a recycled plastic container. The addition of drier carbon-based materials and proper ventilation for airflow will keep your compost balanced under these conditions.

Hot, Dry Climates

Here are tips to prevent a dry compost and rejuvenate a pile in progress:

- Compost should be as moist as a wrung-out rag; thus, if your heap is dry, add water and move the bin into a shady area.
- Keep a lid or tarp over your compost pile to reduce evaporation; dry compost does not decay.
- In a dry climate or during periods of drought, build your compost pile in a container that retains water. Using a plastic barrel or drum is a great idea. Avoid screening, widely spaced slats, and chicken wire because this will promote evaporation. Moisture accumulation from food scraps and heat along the inside of a plastic container will naturally water the contents.
- Make the layers of compost thinner when conditions are dry; you can accomplish this by increasing the surface area—spreading the waste out.
- Every time you add another layer to the organic compost, use the hose to soak the material until it is damp.
- Saturate an old carpet or doormat with water, place it directly on top of the covered pile; repeat each time you add to the pile.
- Arid climates are limited in carbon yard waste such as leaf litter, so add debris like fallen pine needles, wood chips, ashes, corn stalks, shredded newspaper, shredded cardboard, sawdust, straw, and peanut shells.
- When it does rain in your dry climate you'll want to utilize the rainwater: Make the top of the compost indented like a bowl or dish to capture rainwater. Captured water will leach into the depths of the pile versus run off. You can even create a water tube to hydrate the inside of the compost pile. Simply drill holes around a 1" to 2" (3cm–5cm) PVC pipe connected to a water bowl and place it into the center of the pile. When the water flows from the bowl, it is dispersed throughout the center of the pile.

Cold Climates and Winter Composting

There are different ways to look at winter composting depending on your individual goals. Are you interested in keeping an active compost bin or heap through the winter or just wondering what happens to your bin, tumbler, or pile during the winter? Living in the Midwest for example, we have many cold and snowy winter days that may limit our ease in accessing an outdoor compost pile. Ice and snow may even make it impossible to open the lid of our bin. In addition, how will the pile stay warm enough to keep our team of bacteria and fungi and worms alive and active?

Composting in the winter months was confusing to me for the first few seasons. From the very beginning, my understanding of composting was built on the idea that compost needs to be hot to transform. Though this is not entirely true, it is important to keep your compost alive through the winter months if you are intent on achieving a product in early spring. Continuous addition of materials even to an icy pile is necessary to keep it active and alive all winter long. This ensures that you have the necessary bulk to keep a pile warm, and enough food to feed the microorganisms, as well as continuing to reduce your waste stream. Kitchen scraps are available all year round, but yard waste becomes quite scarce in most winter months. Stock pile fall leaves if you intend to keep a winter pile active. It will take quite a lot of materials to insulate the center of the pile and to keep the process of decomposition active. Many compost bins and piles will go dormant for the winter and ignite once again in early spring. Kick-starting with another addition of carbon rich leaves in early spring will be certain to help. This will also absorb much of the moisture from the thaw. If you keep a close eye on the thawing contents early in the spring, you may even get a harvest of compost ready for the first planting of the garden.

Here are some tips for composting in cold climates:

- Place the bin close to an outside wall, alongside the garage or other sheltered area for insulation during cold months.
- Keep your compost in a sunny area to maximize the radiance of the heat of the sun.
- Keep your compost indoors in the winter in a shed or garage.
- Continue adding materials throughout the entire winter season. Remember, the bulk of materials is

essential for the generation of heat. Store some dried leaves in the fall to add a great source of carbon and bulk. When added with your kitchen scraps in the winter, you will keep the bacteria happy and healthy.

- Break down waste into smaller pieces (1"–2" [3cm–5cm] pieces) during the winter to keep the composting process from slowing down excessively. Remember, the smaller the piece, the more surface area, the faster the decomposition takes place.
- In late winter or early spring, when it's too cold outside for worms to come to the surface and enter the pile, you can purchase starter worms to add to your cold compost. Red wigglers will continue working through the center of your compost as long as the temperatures deep within the bin remain above freezing. They will help jump-start the transformation by eating the waste and aerating the compost through their movement.
- Try indoor composting (see chapter 6) during winter months to complement your outdoor efforts. Bokashi systems, indoor worm bins and the NatureMill are great indoor options for winter composting.

Temperate Climates

If you maximize the surrounding resources in your area and control the moisture levels, a temperate climate will easily support your compost.

General rules for composting in a temperate region:

- Sometimes composting can be a challenge in temperate climates due to the unexpected amount of rainwater or temperature variations. Balance the wetness of your heap by adding materials such as hay, sawdust, or leaves.
- If your pile is too wet, remove the lid from the bin for a day or two to allow it to dry out. You can also elevate the compost pile so that the excess liquid can drain from the bottom. Too much liquid can halt the composting process.
- Since most soil is likely to be rich and full of worms, position your compost pile or bin over soil rather than on top of concrete

so worms can freely enter the pile and aid the composting process. Remember, openings in the bottom of a bin allow ventilation, drainage and access to helpful compost assistants (worms and insects).

- When first starting your outdoor compost, toss in a shovelful of fresh soil to introduce an array of soil microorganisms to your bin. Remember, these are the workers that transform your garbage into black gold.

Ventilation

Airflow is essential. It helps to minimize condensation as well as keep the oxygen-dependent microorganisms alive. If moisture levels are not properly balanced with airflow, your closed compost bin may become anaerobic and putrid. This is more likely to occur in a closed container than an outdoor exposed pile or heap. The odor and appearance of the contents under the lid will let you know. As you are assessing your particular needs and choosing a bin, take into account the number and location of ventilation holes. There are some clever ways to create sufficient ventilation while still trying to minimize pest invasions. But, obviously, you should expect that small insects will not be kept out even if squirrels and mice are deterred.

Convenience

If possible, keep your compost in a location that is easy to reach. Throughout the day, the majority of people juggle family, work, and hopefully some hobbies. Time is often of the essence. Although, over time, your composting and gardening may become a hobby and a relaxing activity, it is important to make it convenient in the beginning. Keeping your compost within your general flow of work will help minimize the time and energy needed to maintain it. If possible, keep it close to the kitchen door or on the way to the garage or garbage cans. Make sure that the lid or handles are easy to manage so that you do not have to struggle to add your waste. Locate your compost near a water source to increase the likelihood of maintaining the proper moisture content. Keep additional compost tools (aerating tools, buckets, shovels, and pitchforks) nearby so they are handy when needed.

Appearance

Compost piles, even well maintained ones, can be considered eyesores to many neighbors and family members. A closed bin, tumbler, or hidden trench may be necessary to keep the lawn or landscape unobstructed. For many, the simple cone, tumbler, or ball design of a manufactured compost bin serves this purpose. For others, a trench at the edge of your garden or behind the house may be the key. Burying your compost directly into the ground is a way to camouflage your composting efforts. Keep a trench in an area of your yard that is rarely visited, or create a hidden trench by covering it with wood chips or a plank and a flowerpot. Planting a trellis of climbing flowers in front of your compost is also a great way to hide the plastic or wooden container of your choice. The flowers will benefit from any nutrients that may be leaching through the bottom of a bin as well.

Yield

When choosing a method, you want to establish your goal. Are you engaging in composting to accumulate a product for immediate use in your yard or garden? If so, how patient are you—what is your time line? You may want to choose a faster, more productive method even though it may be a bit more labor intensive. Remember, a hot compost will provide the fastest product. Systems that heat up the fastest require a bulk of materials and frequent turning. A three-bin system (see page 84) provides both of these and may be the best way to create a hot and fast yield if you have the time and space needed.

Are you engaging in composting to lower your carbon footprint and reduce your waste? If so, a system that doesn't yield finished compost, such as the Sun Frost Scrap Eater or Green Cone, may be a good option for you. Both of these methods allow you to continue to add your scraps and require little maintenance on your part. The waste is recycled into the ground below or the plants living within the system.

CHOOSING A COMPOST CONTAINER

There are six main things to consider when selecting a compost container:

1. space available (room for a multiple-bin system, large heap, or compact bin)

2. desired appearance (blend in with surroundings or exposed pile)
3. organic materials available (yard waste, kitchen scraps, leaves, manure)
4. local predators (rats, bears, squirrels, raccoons)
5. cost (low-cost, do-it-yourself, or higher priced manufactured items)
6. regional weather (hot, cold or wet climate)

The Scoop About Poop:
Manure and Compost

Manure is often a great addition to compost. It contains nitrogen, phosphorus, potassium, and many beneficial bacteria that your plants will thrive on. Yet not all poop is the same. Its makeup and benefits in a compost will vary depending on the food source of the animal. If taken from pets that are herbivores, such as rabbits, gerbils, sheep, cows, and

chickens, it acts like an accelerant because of its high level of nitrogen. The addition of this nitrogen-rich form of manure will help heat up a carbon-rich environment or a cold compost quickly.

It is best to use aged manure in your compost. Fresh manure can contain as much as 80 percent water and will affect your pile's moisture levels. In addition, fresh manure can create such intense bacterial activity that it can raise the temperature of the compost too quickly and kill off the earthworms and microbes. Allow manures to age a bit before adding them. Aged manure is drier, a bit lighter in color and less likely to have a strong odor.

Weed seeds may be a consideration when adding manure to your compost. Seeds often make their way through the digestive track of animals and have been known to germinate later on in a pile of manure. This is also possible in your compost. Remember, a hot compost will take care of all seeds, even those added from cow and chicken manures.

Obviously there is a cost to consider when purchasing a prefabricated compost container or the materials to build one. But not to worry, there are many inexpensive methods that work very well, although, there may be trade-offs when selecting less expensive options. For example, no- to low-cost open methods that do not completely contain your matter will not contain the odors occurring during the decomposition as well as a closed method will. It is important to think about your goals for the land in addition to your composting goals.

Size Matters

How much compostable material will you have? How many people are in your household? Will you have compostable garden waste? If, perhaps you don't cook often and you only have a small amount of kitchen scraps, a small digester may be ideal for you. If you have a large yard and garden, you may want a three-bin system so you can compost all of your kitchen and garden waste. Usually, after beginning composting and seeing the benefits, many people can't stand throwing away organic material due to a lack of space in their composting system. Make sure to plan accordingly. Most individuals are shocked to realize just how much waste we accumulate during an average day.

The issue of size may not apply to only the volume of waste your household accumulates. The size of your compost bin is also a factor in its effectiveness and operation in general. Recall that thermophilic bacteria are required to create a hot compost and to get decomposition rolling along. These bacteria require moisture, air, the proper carbon:nitrogen ratio and one more thing: They need space. In order for a pile to heat up, it needs to be at least 3' × 3' (91cm × 91cm) in size (or 3 cubic feet) to adequately raise and hold the proper temperature for a thermophilic breeding ground (104° F to 158° F [40° C to 70° C]).

It is amazing but true: Once this temperature is reached, one could actually boil an egg in the center of the composting materials. Yet if there is not enough space to accumulate the right mix of organic materials, the pile may never be able to reach these temperatures. Many closed bins are not adequate in size to hold the amount of material necessary and, therefore, they may be best used for cold composting.

OUTDOOR COMPOSTING OPTIONS

Compost Bins

Enclosed bin systems, often simply referred to as "composters," are the most common option for outdoor composting today. These are usually fully enclosed apparatus meant to contain your working compost. Most of these bins are manu-

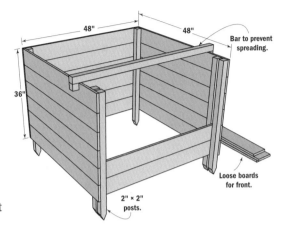

factured using recycled or partially recycled plastic and are commonly seen in black or green. These simple, light-weight structures contain waste and odors while maintaining a neat and ordered appearance. When kept outside in a backyard, the container also deters animals from interfering and keeps excessive amounts of rain off of the compost pile. There are countless commercially available bin systems on the market in a wide variety of shapes, sizes, and price ranges.

The common feature of these various compost bins is their ability to contain your waste within their walls. How each does this and how you access this waste for turning, aerating, adding extra materials, and harvesting your compost may vary from bin to bin. These are additional design elements to familiarize yourself with before making a purchase. Once again, many claims will be made by the manufacturers such as "easy harvesting access," "light weight for easy turning," and "reinforced doors and handles."

Tumblers, orbs, balls, and barrels elevated on frames are a special category of compost bins. These are designed specifically to allow for easier turning and mixing of the contents. By rotating the apparatus, the contents turn, eliminating the need for manual turning with pitchforks and aerating tools. These will be discussed at further length in the tumblers section (page 83) and are a good choice for those who may not be as physically inclined or fit. But be warned, the contents of the bin become quite heavy when moist and still may require a bit of muscle power.

Cones, box-shaped composters, and free standing barrels conversely sit atop the surface of the ground, and are stationary. They, therefore, need additional manpower to mix and aerate the internal contents. These stationary apparatus usually have a door or opening on top to add materials and to access the contents for maintenance. Remember, it is best to turn and aerate your compost regularly to keep the bacteria happy and hot. If your apparatus has a small entry or it is too high for you to easily reach into it with a pitchfork, turning the compost may, ultimately, be difficult. It's best if you think about this before the need arises.

In addition, these stationary bins usually have a small access door at or near the bottom of the apparatus. This door is designed to assist with removal of the lower layers of finished compost. In theory this design is genius. As you continuously add new organic waste to the top of the bin and mix, aerate and let the microbes do their job, you should expect the more finished layers of compost to arrive at the bottom of the bin. Removal from here should be easy. Yet, one of the biggest complaints about stationary composters is how difficult it is to remove their compost. Because this door is small and so low to the ground it is difficult to access with a shovel or hoe. Many prefer to dump the entire contents of their apparatus and separate out the finished compost while returning the processing materials back into the bin. This technique renders the design of the door almost obsolete. Yet, even if removal is challenging, the door may serve another purpose. One of the challenges in a closed-bin apparatus is to see the status of this lower level of materials, due to less visual access. This door may help to determine when your compost is ready.

Because microscopic soil bacteria and wiggly worms play such an important role in composting, many stationary commercial compost bins will have numerous small openings along the bottom surface to invite these local friends to the feast. This open-bottom construction is an important and intentional design feature that can make a significant difference in the speed with which your waste transforms into compost. When considering the purchase of a bin, take this feature into account. When possible, the bottom of a bin should be in direct contact with the Earth. This invites a team of workers into the compost. Worms and microbes will travel through the ground and into your bin to aid in your composting efforts.

Do not be concerned about the access to the natural world below; encourage it! The open-bottom design also allows for excess liquid to drain back into the soil and to allow more generous airflow throughout. Elevated apparatus do not have this feature.

There are many bins on the market in the under-hundred dollar range. These bins are typically made from lighter weight plastic with minimal high-tech features. Some municipalities offer discounts and incentive programs for basic bins to encourage residential composting and to reduce municipal waste. Check with your local extension service or gardening club to see if there are any such programs in your area.

Tumblers

An efficient alternative to the standard stationary compost bin, tumblers are designed for convenience and ease-of-use. Requiring little more than giving the bin a few turns a day, using a compost tumbler is a good option for those looking for a low-maintenance option or for anyone who might not have the physical capacity for turning and aerating a bin by hand. "Tumbler" refers to several different designs, including elevated barrels that rotate on a frame either vertically or horizontally as well as rolling balls or orbs that sit directly on the ground. Aerating

and turning the compost is much quicker with tumblers so they're great for time-crunched people or anyone who is willing to pay a bit more for a system that yields harvestable compost. Some tumbler users indicate that the handles occasionally rust after several seasons of use and that when filled to capacity, a tumbler can be challenging to turn.

The Tumbleweed is a popular tumbler product. It has a 58-gallon (220 liters) capacity, takes about fifteen minutes to assemble and can produce finished compost in as few as twenty-one days when kept at hot-pile temperatures. The Tumbleweed, like most tumblers, is essentially a barrel on legs and is designed for easy spinning. This unit is unique in that it has a stainless steel rod through that center that helps break down material inside the composter as it turns.[1] Hot compost is easier to maintain when the contents are kept aerated and broken down, yet there are some seasoned composters who believe that tumblers and barrels don't have sufficient space to truly heat up efficiently.

Rotating orbs are a relatively new and fun tumbler concept. With these products, the bin is an orb that rolls, rotates, and spins like a ball on the ground. Not only can this be fun for the whole family, it is an efficient way to turn and aerate your compost. The orb eliminates the need to crank a handle or dig into your barrel with a pitchfork or compost aerating tool. These are a wonderful way to get children involved in composting and pets tend to enjoy all the activity as well! Because it uses gravity, it's less strenuous to turn and aerate the compost, yet I have heard that orbs can become quite heavy when full. Another great thing about a rotating orb is that when the compost is finished, you simply roll it to your garden and harvest it—no lifting necessary.

Because of the advanced design, tumblers often cost a bit more than the average composter. Though the cost may be higher, there is still some risk that parts wear out over time and that the lifespan of a tumbler may be limited. Some tumbler users indicate that after several seasons of use the frames are not sturdy enough to handle a full load. In addition, always remember that when filled to capacity, a tumbler can be quite challenging to turn despite its design.

Three-Bin Systems

Three-bin systems allow for composting large quantities of yard and kitchen waste in a short amount of time. Lynn Bement, "The Compost Queen" of Chicago, refers to these as the "Cadillacs of composting." They are sturdy, durable, and attractive. Some are made of wood or plastic slats and can be expanded as needed to meet the needs of your materials. The goal is to build up the contents within the three bins to the proper size

1. "Tumbleweed Compost Tumbler," Clean Air Gardening, www.cleanairgardening.com/patdesaustum.html (accessed April 30, 2010).

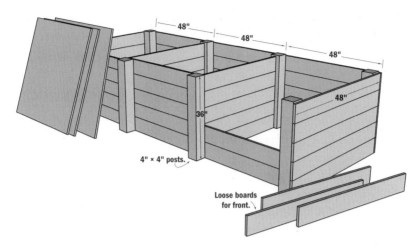

48" 48" 48" 48"

36"

4" × 4" posts.

Loose boards for front.

and mixture to heat up the contents for a hot compost. Some include covers and some are open air. With removable-slat front planks for ease of turning and harvesting, these systems make transferring various levels of materials between bins easy while generally containing matter for aesthetics. More than one bin allows you to have a bin for the pile being built (as ingredients are accumulated over a period of time) and two more for piles in more advanced stages of decomposition. If you have the space for such a system, and are generating or gathering enough materials to keep the bins in use, this can be very convenient. Having three compartments allows you turn the compost regularly from one compartment into the next, keeping two piles cooking at all times. Usually, by the time you're ready to start a third one, it's time to empty the first bin and work it into a garden bed.

When using a three-bin system, some people start with the left bin. Then when it's time to begin another pile, the original pile is turned into the middle bin, which aerates it and accelerates the composting process. A new pile is then built in the left-most bin. When that pile is completed, the old pile in the middle is turned a final time into the right-most bin for finishing, and the newest pile is turned into the middle bin, making the left-most bin available for yet another pile. Then the finished compost will eventually be removed from the right-most bin.

Specialty Compost Bins

The Earthmaker is a popular 124-gallon (469 liters) stationary compost bin retailing for about $249. This system looks like a basic stationary bin but it has "dents" in the side, which work to separate the bin into three chambers, allowing for three stages of decomposition. It's essentially akin to a three-bin system, but in a single bin! As you learn more about composting, you will clearly see the benefit of separating the stages of decay. Initial decomposition starts in the top chamber. After three to five weeks, the compost is transferred to the second chamber by sliding out a panel. This frees up the top bin for new kitchen and yard waste. After another three to five weeks, the compost is moved from the second to the third chamber and at the same time, the compost in the top chamber will be ready for the second chamber. After further decomposition, the compost in the third chamber can be harvested for use from a ground-level door. The three-chamber design allows for continuous composting in a single bin and produces a finished product quicker than the traditional one-chamber bin systems. Yet, the compact design allows for full containment and requires less space than the three-bin system on page 85.

The Sun Frost Scrap Eater is one of the more unique offerings. This ingenious "living machine" doubles as a planter as well as a composter. If that's not cool enough, it's also made out of an attractive and recycled oak Bordeaux wine barrel. Food scraps are composted in a sealed environment so you can place the Scrap Eater in any sunny location, such as a deck, patio, or balcony without the worry of odor, insects, or animals.

A plastic dome on top collects heat and the insulated chamber traps it, making the Scrap Eater a solar-powered composter. The dome also channels water to the plants around the perimeter of the barrel as well as inside the chamber, keeping the pile moist. When the plants growing on the composter mature, they will extend their roots to the bottom of the compost chamber and directly extract nutrients and moisture from the composted food scraps. This process continues the natural cycle much like it occurs in nature.

The Scrap Eater can be used to rapidly compost large batches of food scraps at once but is typically used by adding small amounts of scraps every few days, comfortably processing scraps from two-to-four people. The company does not recommend composting meat, dairy, bones, etc. The speed of decomposition decreases as the chamber fills up. With the right C:N ratio, this unit can reach temperatures as high as 150° F (66° C).

The Scrap Eater can also be used for vermiculture, however, the compost chamber will typically be 30° F (-1° C) above the ambient temperature and during the summer may be too hot for the worms, which will encourage the worms to migrate to the cooler perimeter where the plants are growing.

The Scrap Eater produces very little compost, making it a drawback for some and a benefit for others. If you simply want a convenient alternative to tossing organic waste in the garbage, but don't necessarily want a yield of compost, this system might be a good solution for you. Another potential drawback of this system is cost. For the ease-of-use, neat design and attractiveness, you can expect to pay a few hundred dollars for one of these systems.

The Green Johanna Hot Komposter is another commercially available bin system. This insulated, rodent-proof bin allows for year-round composting in most climates. (The company also offers a "winter jacket" for use north of the 40th latitude, which includes Boulder, Colorado, and Toledo, Ohio.) This system is completely self-contained and can maintain a high temperature for accelerated decomposition. Because the bin is constructed with a double layer of plastic, it is more pest resistant and can maintain high

Photo Courtesy of abundantearth.com.com

temperatures for quick decomposition. Holes in the base allow drainage and encourage worms, insects, bacteria, and fungi to enter freely. Like a traditional barrel or ball compost bin, the Green Johanna composts paper and organic kitchen scraps. The company also encourages placement of all types of food waste, including meat, fish, bones, and oil-soaked leftovers. Of course, these recommendations should be considered by each individual household. There's no guarantee that composting this wide array of materials will be trouble-free during cooler times of the year. Problems such as odor and slow decomposition may discourage you.

The system is sized for kitchen scraps from a family of up to five people along with garden waste. The Green Johanna requires aerating as well as the proper C:N ratio of greens and browns. The company recommends placing it in the shade to avoid overheating. Because of its durability and insulated walls, you can expect to pay a few hundred dollars for this bin.

Many individuals will store large bulk amounts of carbon based materials in one of the bins for easy use when building on the C:N ratio. Unless you build it yourself, three-bin systems can be pricey. Materials to make your own will cost between one and two hundred dollars. An even less expensive way to make your own is to recycle shipping pallets.

Digesters

Digesters, also sometimes referred to as universal composters, are a great low-maintenance option, and many digester systems take all food waste including meat, bones, and dairy. These hot systems consist of an above-ground, semi-enclosed bin that's usually insulated with a top opening for depositing food scraps. Some digesters are either open on the bottom or have a vented bottom basket that's buried underground. The black gold simply seeps out the bottom once digested, greatly reducing the need to regularly turn or even harvest the compost. Some digester systems only require harvesting every two years, if at all. Except for the top, the above-ground portion of the digester system is completely enclosed and therefore doesn't attract hungry critters like rats and squirrels.

The Green Cone is one example of a digester compost product that's commercially available. An above-ground, double-walled plastic cone uses solar radiation to create a heat trap of circulating air, which encourages the thermophiles. It also provides insulation in the winter for year-round use in most climates.

A below-ground chamber invites worms and microorganisms to migrate in and out of the basket. Unlike outdoor compost bins, you can add meat, bones, pet waste, dairy, and processed foods to these digesters because they get hot enough to kill the pathogens and pests cannot access it.[2]

2. "An Indepth Look," Solarcone, http://solarcone.net/system/in_depth.php (accessed April 27, 2010).

But, partially due to its small size, it is not designed for composting garden waste and the contents should not be turned or aerated. Green Cones run between one and two hundred dollars, which seems relatively reasonable considering it's a hot-pile option that is low-maintenance.

Install digesters in a sunny location with good drainage—you don't want any water to collect near a digester. You can put plants near your digester and they will have the dual benefit of disguising it and taking advantage of the nutrients that leach out from the bottom. However, you won't want to place it near edible plants or veggies if you're using it for pet waste.

Digesters are a great composting option for people who want an outdoor system but don't want to spend a lot of time dealing with a compost pile and aren't looking for much, if any, compost yield. At the same time, digesters complement bin systems nicely and some, like the Green Cone, can be a good option for people who want to compost more items because they take meat, dairy, and pet excrement.

Piles or Heaps

Simple is often better, despite what the marketing companies repeatedly tell us. A pile, or heap, of organic waste is a preferred method of composting that dates back before the invention of recycled plastic backyard tumblers and bins. Heaps are ideal for those who tend towards simpler lifestyles and anyone with sufficient outdoor space. Minimal or no store-bought equipment is needed to build or operate a compost pile or heap.

Creating a composting heap is quick, easy, and cheap. Here are some simple directions to get you going:

1. Select a dry, shady spot near a water source.
2. Start with a 4" to 6" (10cm–15cm) layer of browns on the bottom. You can even use sticks and coarse materials for better aeration.
3. Mix grass clippings and other green waste into the pile and bury fruit and vegetable waste under 10" (25cm) of compost material.
4. Add your brown and green materials as you collect them. Chopping or shredding large pieces will speed up decomposition.
5. You may want to moisten dry materials as they are added if your heap tends to dry out.

6. Optional: Cover the top of compost with a tarp to keep it moist.

7. When the material at the bottom is dark and rich in color, your compost is ready to use (this can occur anytime between two months to two years).[3]

Unless you cover your heap, it is going to be exposed to animals and to the elements. That means you definitely don't want to include meat, bones, dairy, or fish to keep critters away. Covering the nitrogen-rich materials with browns will help to keep away unwanted scavengers as well.

DO-IT-YOURSELF COMPOSTERS
Barrel Tumblers

There are several popular plans for building your own tumbler. Some incorporate complex bases and turning mechanisms others suggest a platform with wheels. The simplest way is to use an old barrel and two recycled tires. Instructions:

1. Cut a rectangular hole in the side of a plastic barrel using a jigsaw. Size the hole so it's not too big, as it will have to carry considerable weight when rolling the full bin around, however, it needs to be big enough to get a rake or shovel into—about 20" long × 8" wide (51cm × 20cm) is a good starting point.

2. Attach the door with two large pivot hinges and then create a locking closure with a pin lock.

3. Drill ten to twenty, ½" (13mm) holes all around for aeration and drainage.

4. Lay one tire on the ground. Center the barrel on top of the tire and draw around it with a marker. Remove the barrel.

5. Drill a couple of holes in the tire. Then fit a saw through the holes and cut close to the steel belt all the way around. This is a way to get the steel belts out because it's impossible to saw through them.

6. Put the barrel inside the tire

7. Repeat steps 5 and 6 for the second tire.

3. "Create Your Own Compost Pile," U.S. Environmental Protection Agency, www.epa.gov/osw/conserve/rrr/composting/by_compost.htm (accessed May 18, 2010).

Bins

You can make your own bin using a regular garbage can, although it may not have all of the benefits of a store-bought one. Galvanized or plastic cans can be used, but a tight-fitting lid is essential to keep odors in and critters out.

Instructions:

1. Drill or punch about twenty drain holes, ¼" to ⅜" (6mm–10mm) in diameter in the bottom of the can.
2. Then, drill twenty more side holes on the lower third of the can.
3. In a well-drained location, dig a hole about half as deep as your container; set the can into the hole, making sure all of the vent holes are buried, and push the soil back in around the sides of the can.

Wire Mesh Enclosures

Aside from a simple heap, wire compost bins are probably the simplest and least expensive way to build a large and effective compost. A wire-mesh holding unit is inexpensive and easy to build out of chicken wire. Compared to an uncontained heap, the wire will help keep the compost in place while building the contents to a sufficient size for hot composting. Wire mesh also allows for good airflow throughout the compost. Wire is capable of holding itself upright and can be used alone, or posts can be added to stabilize the container. A wire-mesh bin made without posts is easy to lift and provides simple access to the finished compost at the bottom of the pile while the compost at the top of the pile is still decomposing.

Instructions:

1. Using a 10' (30m) piece of 36" (91cm) wide chicken wire, fold back 3" to 4" (8cm–10cm) at each end to create a strong, clean edge that will not poke or snag and will be easy to latch.
2. Stand the wire in a circle and set it in place for the compost pile.
3. Using pliers, cut pieces of heavy-duty wire into lengths for ties and latch the ends of the chicken wire together.
4. If using posts, space them around the inside of the chicken-wire circle. Position the posts tightly against the wire and pound them firmly into the ground for support.

The Humanure Project

Although most of the world's human waste, a.k.a. "humanure," is quickly flushed down the drain or discarded into the environment as a pollutant, some people are converting it into nutrient-rich fertilizer through composting.

The Humanure Handbook, by Joseph C. Jenkins, began as a master's thesis project for a Science in Sustainable Systems program in the 1990s. Since then, humanure composting has gained quite a following. Now in its third edition, *The Humanure Handbook* has sold tens of thousands of copies since it was first published in 1995. Not only has Jenkins received loads of press coverage and administrates an active online discussion forum, but the author also travels to developing countries to help communities develop environmentally and financially sustainable alternative sanitation systems.[4]

Proponents of humanure composting have redefined human waste and instead of waste, consider it fertilizer for the soil. Nance Klehm, horticultural consultant and permaculture grower in Chicago, would probably agree. Klehm is the mastermind behind the "Humble Pile Chicago" project where she enlisted twenty-two neighbors to stop using their toilets and save their waste in five-gallon buckets. Over a three-month period, Klehm retrieved the humanure and when the process is complete, she will supply the participants with their share of the humanure compost. Klehm says that a coliform test showed zero detectable fecal bacteria in the resulting compost.[5]

Humanure is essentially composted using an outdoor bin system. Instead of a flushing toilet, humanure composters use a wooden box with a hole in the top and a 5-gallon bucket below to collect the deposits. Of course, a toilet seat is added for comfort and familiarity as well. Each deposit is covered with sawdust, which eliminates worrisome odors as well as controls excess moisture. When the bucket is full, the toilet material is emptied into an outdoor bin and covered with "brown" material such as straw. Food scraps are typically composted in the same bin. The temperature is carefully monitored to ensure it reaches proper temperature to kill any pathogens, and precautions are taken in the bin design and when depositing material to prevent leaching. Then the pile "rests" inactive (with no additional deposits) for at least one year before being harvesting for the compost.[6] The resulting rich compost is definitely not the same product it started out as.

Proponents of composting human waste are not advocating spreading human feces on the garden similar to the Chinese "night soils." The thermophilic bacteria hard at work in a compost pile will convert the human waste into an agricultural product. It has been suggested that no other method of human waste processing achieves this without harmful chemicals and extreme energy consumption.

Humanure composting is an excellent option for people in rural and remote areas. However, increasing numbers of urbanites are choosing to compost humanure for the environmental benefits. Not only does the resulting compost nourish the soil and plants, it also reduces the burden on municipal waste treatment plants and, as a result, reduces the resources required for the treatment process—water, energy, and chemicals.

The Loveable Loo is available as a kit or fully assembled. Photos courtesy of Joseph Jenkins, www.humanurehandbook.com.

4. & 6. Joseph Jenkins, Humanure Headquarters, www.humanurehandbook.com (accessed April 22, 2010).

5. Adam Fisher, "Humanure: Goodbye, Toilets. Hello, Extreme Composting," *Time*, 4 December 2009.

COMPOSTING WITHOUT EQUIPMENT

Now that you have everything you need to know about composting equipment and various specialty apparatus, consider composting without equipment at all. Not only are there low-cost methods of outdoor composting, there are methods to compost throughout the yard, below the surface or right on top of it. Both trench or pit composting and lasagna composting are simple, effective, and inexpensive methods to add nutrients to your soil and minimize waste.

Trench

Trench composting may be the ideal system for people who have garden space but don't want to fuss with bins and piles. It is the ultimate in low-maintenance composting. It's also invisible and odor-free. Incidentally, trench composting is also the final step in Bokashi composting.

Simply bury your chopped kitchen wastes in an 8" (20cm) trench. The trench can be as long as you like, but the depth should be at least 8" (20cm) to keep animals from digging up the food scraps. After you bury the materials, they will begin to decompose with the help of soil microbes. Within several months this garden soil will be ready for planting. There's no need to harvest your compost from the trench. Simply plant directly on top of this nutrient-rich earth. The plant roots will thrive. You may consider trenching along the back edge of an existing garden to add nutrients to the area throughout the growing season.

Another form of trench composting is a pit with a lid. This option provides a long-term, below-ground option for your waste disposal while keeping a "lid" on the odors. Ease of use is key here. Dig a large pit and cover it with a simple lid such as a piece of plywood anchored with rocks. No need to shovel dirt on top of newly placed materials. Mixing new organic materials with those already in the pit will hasten the decomposition process. Though harvesting from a pit is not essential, it can be quite simple as all you need to do is shovel out the finished material.

Lasagna

Also known as "sheet composting," lasagna composting, like most other methods of composting, involves layering browns and greens. However, it is done in the location where you would eventually add harvested compost. A form of passive composting, the lasagna method requires a minimum amount of labor. Lasagna composting is an excellent way to prepare a new garden site.

Instructions:

1. Cut any plants growing on the selected area to ground level.
2. Cover the area with layers of corrugated cardboard and newspaper.
3. Add a layer of manure and begin alternating layers of green and brown materials.
4. If you do not have access to manure, continue to layer organic waste (greens) with newspaper and cardboard (browns). The soil microbes will still have a great feast!

You can keep building your compost to a height of a foot or more. Some people cover the pile with a layer of straw for aesthetics. Decomposition takes time, so the best time to lasagna compost is in fall so it's ready the following spring or early summer. By that time, the organic materials will have smothered the roots of plants previously growing on the site and the materials will have decomposed enough to be worked into the soil.

6: Indoor Composting?

> "At this moment in history, we are all caught in the hell of frenetic passivity."
>
> —R.D. Laing

The revelation that composting can be done indoors changed my life. There was no longer a reason to be passive in the composting arena. As a longtime urban dweller, who often had little access to a plot of grass or even a balcony, I had never even considered exploring composting. Why would I? At the time, I didn't have anywhere to put a large bin, I had no garden to fertilize, and it sounded quite labor-intensive and complicated. Even if I was able to figure out the necessary carbon:nitrogen ratio, what was I going to do with the resulting compost? I only had a couple of houseplants and I wasn't very skilled with keeping them happy, so I thought I would surely have more compost than they would need. Sound familiar?

Yes, it really is true: Composting can be done indoors. This is still a revolutionary idea to many individuals, especially for urban dwellers. Has the image of a fruit fly infested, stinky garbage can on a hot summer day come to mind? Erase this image; no one should be asked to endure putrid odors in their home. There are several odorless ways to transform organic materials into valuable and useful humus in the comforts of your home, apartment, condo, garage, or basement.

When I met "the worms" in my friend's kitchen in Berkeley, California, I was in for a shock. Not only were there perfectly good ways to compost inside in a small space, I also realized that composting is not just about creating a better garden; its about creating a better planet. As if a light turned on in a dark room, I realized that composting isn't all about what I need or what I have; it is about an activity that could enhance my life and the lives of future generations. Minimizing our waste and feeding Mother Earth is not just a job for suburbanites or farmers—it can be a way of life for all of us. Composting can be done anywhere! The worms were my first experience of indoor composting, and now I have found multiple methods to suit the needs of multiple lifestyles.

If the question still remains—as it often does during discussion about composting—"What would I do with the compost? I don't have a garden," believe me, compost, and worm castings specifically, are a hot commodity. I wouldn't be surprised if you choose to extend your green thumb further

Yes, it really is true, composting can be done indoors.

once you see the rich, earthy product, like I did. After seeing the amazing natural process of transforming garbage into soil, chances are, you will want to start a window box or herb garden. But if not, a friend or neighbor would probably love to take it off your hands. Organic compost costs a pretty penny at the local garden shop. You may even be able to sell your product and make a few extra bucks to invest in those great organic vegetables at the farmers' markets. Plus, the amount of waste that enters a worm bin is exponentially reduced in volume while it is being transformed into humus. The resulting compost is not overflowing; it is a manageable amount and a valuable product.

BENEFITS OF COMPOSTING INDOORS

There are many reasons why composting indoors may be appealing. Indoor methods allow everyone the opportunity to participate in composting, the cycle of life, and active waste stream reduction, regardless of their living situation. The approaches may differ in scale and process, but they still produce a beautiful product for use with houseplants, window boxes, and larger outdoor gardens. These methods are easy and clean, and they encourage the entire household to take part in mindful behavior. Indoor methods of composting generally take up less physical space and are designed to minimize odors while efficiently transforming waste. As an added benefit, the physical effort required to maintain an indoor system is often significantly less compared to outdoor systems because there's no turning required. The output is usually produced in smaller batches with less physical maintenance and the travel time to the composter is usually much shorter.

Another clear advantage to indoor composting methods, and possibly the most relevant, is that you can easily maintain your practice of collection and waste stream reduction year round, no matter how cold it is outside. You will never have to traipse out to the compost pile or bin in the dead of winter to deposit your scraps, definitely a benefit for many! The most common complaint that I hear from people here in Chicago is that their outdoor tumbler or pile stalls out in the winter. Some people continue to pile on the kitchen scraps throughout the winter if ice and snow do not sabotage their efforts, but there is very little bacterial activity going in the cold season. Although we have a beautiful summer, the warm season is limited and so is the possibility of creating a hot compost pile year round. And boy does that cold pile take a long time to transform itself into usable compost if left to struggle though a Chicago winter!

THE NOSE KNOWS

To be widely accepted, indoor composting needs to minimize odor. Your mother was right: There are good reasons to avoid keeping old food in the house! Yet, with thought and intention, composting indoors can be done without putrid odors and slimy, fly-infested cans. Most indoor composting units utilize variations on the traditional decomposition process of an outdoor bin. For instance, in a worm bin, the worms eat your garbage; it doesn't, by definition, decompose. In a Bokashi bucket system, your waste is fermented, like good wine. Both have a reduced risk for odor-producing bacteria, and they eliminate the skills needed to control the often tricky carbon:nitrogen (C:N) ratio that eludes many first-time (as well as long-standing) composters. These two methods do not rely on the heat to keep the bacteria happy, hungry, and decomposing.

One indoor method does rely on the mid- and high-temperature bacteria for organic material transformation. But, this electric kitchen appliance, named NatureMill, has been intelligently designed to hasten the process through an added heat source as well as a sealed system to minimize odors.

The idea of having food waste kept inside the home can be difficult for many to imagine due to the cultural emphasis placed on modern day antibacterial soaps and industrial cleansers. Once you start composting indoors, a shift in the perception and definition of cleanliness and

Bacteria and fungi working with us are more natural than the chemical cleaners we use to sterilize our lives.

garbage takes place. We quickly remember that these bacteria and fungi working indoors are more natural than the chemical cleaners we use to sterilize our lives.

THE PERFECT PAIRING

Many individuals, including myself, maintain an outdoor compost heap and a complementary method of indoor composting. Doing this often simplifies the work and maximizes waste stream reduction. Utilizing an indoor method easily manages most kitchen scraps and leftovers while the outdoor heap fills with yard waste (grass, leaves, spent vegetable stalks). Indoor waste is transported to the indoor receptacle of choice, and your outdoor bin will be close at hand when you are out in the yard caring for your lawn and garden. When a dinner party or family reunion fills the indoor worm bin with scraps, you will have the outdoor barrel or tumbler for overflow as well.

When I develop a new habit and keep up with it, it becomes natural. When I work hard at my outdoor compost in the spring and summer and then watch it freeze over in the winter, I become a bit disillusioned, and I am not alone. I have heard it from the best of the urban homesteaders that they just collect their scraps through the winter until the bin is full, and then give up until spring. This doesn't have to be the case because there are some great methods to keep you composting year round. Not only that, by composting year round, you are storing up the product of your efforts until spring when you are ready to start the garden, if you so choose. The winter is the perfect time to prepare your compost and have it ready for early spring seedlings and landscaping.

INDOOR COMPOSTING METHODS

Indoor composting methods include NatureMill, an electric indoor composting device, Bokashi indoor composting systems, and vermicomposting bins (worm bins). Exploring and understanding the similarities and differences will help you to make the best decision for your particular lifestyle.

NatureMill Automatic Compost Bin

The NatureMill automatic compost bin is essentially a standard kitchen appliance that composts. It's compact, low-maintenance, and no installation required. You simply plug it into a standard outlet. The company also offers a cabinet kit so you also have the option of concealing it in a cabinet, but that does require some installation. The trade-off for the convenience and ease-of-use of this method is cost. The units range in price from $299 to $399 each. If cost is not a strong concern, this may be a good choice for a busy lifestyle.

Photo Courtesy of naturemill.com

The fact that the device runs on electricity has been a concern to many urban homesteaders unwilling to make energy trade-offs for convenience. Although it's true that spending excessive amounts of energy to create compost conflicts with the green movement, the company claims that the NatureMill uses the same amount of electricity as a night light. The increased energy consumption is minimal when using this convenient indoor device and fits the lifestyle of many. A question to ask is: Is it worth using a small amount of energy in order to reduce the amount of waste that I contribute to a landfill and to supply our depleted soil with much-needed nutrients?

Similar only to a Bokashi system (page 102), this composter accepts just about all kitchen scraps, including meat, fish, and dairy. These items are often kept out of outdoor bins because of the odors that attract hungry animals and the risk of pathogenic bacteria at cold composting temperatures. The guaranteed and consistent high heat generated in the NatureMill system breaks those items down in a relatively short period of time and odors are minimal thanks to the airtight design. This is a real benefit to many meat eaters. Although these guaranteed high temperatures would be expected to break down more fibrous materials as well, the NatureMill is not perfect. Hard or fibrous materials, such as bones, paper, corncobs, and corn husks can cause the machine to jam, which is a common complaint from new users until they become more familiar with the machine.

With this system you can add up to 120 pounds (54kg) of material per month, close to four pounds (2kg) per day, and receive compost within a speedy two weeks! Because this machine heats the compost to 140° F (60° C), it has even been suggested that the high temperatures make it safe to compost pet waste and kitty litter along with meat, dairy, and bones. Despite these claims, I feel like we have more to learn in this area, and I am not yet 100 percent comfortable recommending that we compost this pet waste. There are some important considerations, including bacterial infections, residual medications, and disease processes that exist in domesticated animal waste that may interfere with the safety of utilizing the compost, especially on edible gardens.

To use the NatureMill, simply open the drawer and add your food scraps to the mixing chamber. For proper balance, the NatureMill system requires the addition of sawdust for the brown component and baking soda to reduce acidity. For every five cups of food scraps (green material), the instructions state to add one cup of sawdust pellets and one tablespoon of baking soda. Although, some NatureMill users recommend adding closer to a one-and-a-half to two-parts brown to four-parts green to truly keep odors away. Just like with all composting systems, if there's a particularly unpleasant odor, then something's wrong. The most common error in using this system is not adding enough brown in the compost mix. Fortunately, this is a simple problem to fix, and you will quickly determine the ratio that works best for you.

An internal motor, which is reported to be noisy until it breaks in, heats and mixes the compost every four hours. Within forty-eight hours the compost will start to look granular and moist and have an earthly odor. Once the compost gets to this stage and the mixing chamber is full, you simply push a button and the machine transfers it to a lower tray where it continues to compost. When full, the lower tray slides out revealing your black gold. Simply remove the product and apply to houseplants, the lawn and garden, or store it for future use.

Relatively low-maintenance, the mixer and exterior can be cleaned with a damp towel and the trays are simply rinsed out. Handle the trays with care; users note that trays are a bit fragile for long-term use. An air filter deep inside the unit needs to be replaced every five years. If there is one significant downfall to an apparatus of this high-tech nature it is that it can malfunction, need replacement parts, or just stop working. Though the reviews are favorable overall, this is the replacement age of electronics and this device is electronic.

Bokashi Bucket Composting

What is Bokashi? Now that you know much more about the process of aerobic decomposition taking place in outdoor composting methods as well as the NatureMill system, you will understand that a different process is used in Bokashi composting. It relies on bacteria that thrive in an oxygen-free zone to transform waste. Other forms of composting discussed so far rely heavily on the presence of oxygen. Bokashi doesn't because it is a process of fermentation. For all practical purposes, Bokashi pickles our garbage. During the pickling of waste, oxygen is not needed.

In previous chapters, you learned that the sign of an anaerobic compost bin is a putrid smell when taking off the lid, a sure sign of a problem

Photo: Jenny Harlen www.bokashi.se

that needs to be addressed. Because you are now recruiting anaerobic bacteria to do our work through the fermentation process in Bokashi composting, ensuring an airtight environment is essential. Although this receptacle is kept in an anaerobic, airtight state, it does not emit a putrid odor. I won't go as far as to say there is no odor when the lid is removed to add additional waste, but the odor is rather sweet or sour, similar to soy sauce. Even if this sweet-sour odor is less than desirable to you, the bucket receptacle is designed to be airtight for effectiveness and for the prevention of odors.

Fermenting Garbage? It is not the airtight environment alone that leads to fermented garbage. It is the effective microorganisms (EM) that are applied with each new kitchen waste addition. As with other compost-ing methods, you create the proper environment for the team you are trying to recruit. To do that in a Bokashi system, you apply what looks like a simple bag of bran, such as Bokashi compost starter, which is a dry mixture of bran and molasses that has been inoculated with EM. These effective microorganisms are a carefully controlled mixture of microscop-ic bacteria, yeasts, and fungi that work together to speed up compost-ing, suppress pathogens, prevent putrefaction, and eliminate foul odors.

Part of the reason these particular microbial communities work so well indoors is that they do not allow odoriferous gasses to form.

When we pickle food, such as cucumbers and beets, for our consumption, we are ensuring a safe and extended period of preservation. Food lasts longer without the risk of harmful pathogens taking over. Bokashi composting follows a similar concept. Although it would not be wise to plan to serve up a meal from the Bokashi bucket, it is a safe way to contain aging food and organic matter. The types of microbes that are harmful to us cannot survive in the acidic environment created in fermentation.

Bokashi is one of the most easily maintained systems for composting kitchen scraps. To use a Bokashi system, you simply add your kitchen scraps to an airtight bucket manufactured for this purpose and then cover them with a handful of the compost starter containing the microorganisms. Kits containing these buckets as well as the starter bags of effective microorganisms are available online. I recommend adding waste once

Some Bokashi experts say that the liquid gold acts as a natural drain cleaner. The enzymes within the liquid by-product will eat right through the buildup within your old pipes.

daily to minimize the exposure to air within the bucket and the need for compost starter. By collecting waste and adding it at the end of the day, you use one large handful of microorganisms. In addition, as with many other forms of composting, cutting scraps up into small pieces speeds up the fermentation process. Surface area is increased when the food scraps are cut smaller. Both the breakdown and fermentation process are accelerated by increased surface area. To ensure that you maintain an airtight environment, press the new food waste down with a plate or piece of cardboard to remove trapped air within the particles. Repeat this procedure every time you add scraps. Remember, this system is capable of taking all of your kitchen waste, oils, fish bones, meats, dairy products, and hot peppers.

When the bucket is full, drain the liquid from the spigot near the base of the unit and allow the contents to ferment for seven to ten days. This period of time is needed to continue the anaerobic process of fermentation, ensuring a quick transformation of the waste to soil compost once buried outside. After seven to ten days have passed, check for any remaining liquid drainage and drain off this liquid. Remove the contents from the bucket and bury outside in the soil where complete breakdown occurs within two to three weeks. Bokashi composting does not completely degrade all material within the bucket; it retains much of its physical appearance and will look pickled, even when you are burying it. It is the soil microorganisms that take over from here. They will work rapidly to break down the remaining contents of your fermented waste. This fermented waste will actually turn to soil within the earth. As it transforms, it feeds the surrounding plants, the soil food web, and Mother Earth herself. All of this occurs within those first two to three weeks in the ground.

Unlike many composting systems, you do not harvest a finished compost product for use around the house. When you bury the pickled waste, you are giving the nutrients back to the soil to be used where they are buried. When planned well, you can trench (see the section on trench composting in chapter 5) your Bokashi contents right into the edge of your garden or flower bed for use by the plants and soil where they are needed. As the fermented scraps breakdown and transform, the roots of neighboring plants will be fed over time. If gardening is not your goal, a deep hole, prepared trench, or pit can be used to discard the waste repeatedly over time. A hole should be at least 12" (30cm) deep to discourage local pests from becoming curious.

It is not recommended to immediately plant directly over newly buried Bokashi waste, due to the high level of acid in the contents. Within two to three weeks after depositing your Bokashi waste, the soil will be have transformed sufficiently to support new planting directly on top.

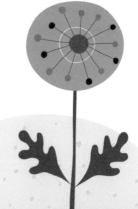

Chicago-based Bokashi expert and urban farmer and educator Seneca Kern routinely utilizes this form of indoor composting with his clients of WeFarm, a residential organic urban farming company. Kern and his staff encourage

Bokashi composting as a way to help maintain a healthy organic garden. To ensure year-round composting, Kern advocates preparing a trench in the late fall before the final freeze and covering it with a tarp so that Bokashi waste can continue to be deposited year-round. By trenching the waste and covering it with a pile of prepared soil, even in the winter, you are perfectly poised for spring planting. By the time the spring roles in, that trench is full of nutrient-rich soil that's ready to support plant growth. Not only are Bokashi composting households growing their own food, they are growing their own soil as well!

If you are partnering up an indoor method of composting and an outdoor bin or tumbler, you can also add your Bokashi contents directly to your outdoor compost. The scraps will go through the final stages buried deep within the composting yard waste as well. Some say that worms will consume Bokashi waste, but I do not recommend depositing large amounts of the fermented waste into a worm bin all at once. This may be too acidic for the worms and overload them with fermented food.

A typical Bokashi bucket holds 5 gallons (19 liters) and will fit under most kitchen sinks. The obvious advantages to such a small, contained system is clear: minimal travel time to and from collection source (the kitchen), no putrid odors, and no unsightly apparatus to contend with. There's no need to recruit the wigglers in this approach to composting. So anyone who may be squeamish about worms can just let them do their magic in your garden naturally.

Although you can build your own bucket system out of a 5-gallon (19 liters) plastic bucket, the Bokashi buckets sold at retail outlets are very well designed and not too expensive. Buckets are usually plastic, often recycled, and always airtight to ensure an ideal environment for anaerobic fermentation to take place, while controlling odors and deterring flies. Most systems have an interior strainer or tray to separate the solid from the liquid that accumulates at the bottom of the bucket. A drainage spout is handy for harvesting the liquid gold.

Just as black gold refers to finished compost, liquid gold refers to the valuable golden-colored liquid that is drained off of a Bokashi bucket during the process of fermentation. This liquid is a solution of living beneficial microbes, enzymes, and rich nutrients and is also an amazing soil and house plant amendment when diluted with water. Some Bokashi experts say that the liquid gold acts as a natural drain cleaner as well. The enzymes within the liquid gold by-product will eat right through the buildup within your old pipes. Pour some of it down your drains regularly instead of harsh chemical drain cleaners and keep your drains running freely.

Perhaps one of the negatives of using a Bokashi system is the need to replace the compost starter mix. It is necessary to use it every time you add scraps to the system. That is why it is a good idea to add waste once daily as opposed to every meal preparation. Bokashi compost starter microorganisms can be found online and run about ten to fifteen dollars for a two-pound (1kg) bag, which should last one to two months. It is possible to make your own Bokashi mix if you wish. There are plenty of instructions available on the Internet if you are interested in giving that a try.

While the system is perfect for an apartment or condo from a size perspective, many smaller residential units do not have access to an outdoor space for burial. If that's true for your situation, ask a friend or family member if they are willing to accept your waste. A few of my clients have deposited their fermenting Bokashi waste into a specially designated enclosed receptacle such as a garbage can. This is not to be thrown away at this stage, but kept aside for the transformation. Covered with soil or dried leaves within a receptacle, the fermentation process will continue resulting in valuable compost. Remember, the fermentation prepares the waste for the soil microbes to take over. If you use a receptacle, then just add the microbes. Even without a garden, it's easy to find a home for this rich compost. The important factor is to have an adequate amount of soil in the container to bury and completely cover the waste. It is the active soil microorganisms that are actually making the change at this stage of the composting and the added coverage of dirt is essential to complete the process.

Vermicomposting With Worm Bins

Ever since my introduction to worm composting in Berkeley, California, I have held a special place in my heart for my team of red wiggler composting worms. My adventures as Urban Worm Girl started because of these amazing little creatures and the wisdom they hold. Since then, I felt I needed to share all that I learned with those around me. The world has not looked the same since I saw these little guys at work. Bette Midler commented in a *Los Angeles Times* interview, "My whole life has been spent waiting for an epiphany, a manifestation of God's presence, the kind of transcendent, magical experience that lets you see your place in the big picture. And that is what I had with my first compost heap." This connection to the divine was reinforced to me through my exposure to the worms and their role in composting and soil building.

On a practical note, a worm bin is one of the simplest and most effective methods of indoor composting available. Whether building your own bin or purchasing a commercially available model, the results of vermicomposting can be amazing. Housing thousands of wiggly worms within your home may not have been in your plans, but it should be. "A worm bin in every home" is Urban Worm Girl's slogan for the future.

Thousands of worms in your kitchen—what a crazy idea! Well, the amazing red wiggler worm is one of the most natural and efficient home composters. They are also very quiet, do not need to be taken for a walk, and don't need paid vacation time off. These amazing little creatures work (eat) long hours without a fight. Recruiting these fellows to consume your organic waste, paper products, and coffee grounds is one of the easiest ways, to be successful at composting even in a small studio apartment or a condominium without a yard. Worm bins can be fabricated or purchased in various sizes to accommodate small spaces.

Worms are part of the natural recycling process occurring along the surface of the earth on a daily basis. Recruiting worms into our home as composters is distinctly different from basic outdoor composting methods and from simply adding worms to an outdoor compost bin or tumbler to accelerate the decomposition occurring within. Worm composting bins are structures for worms to live in while they actually eat your garbage. The process of decomposition in vermicomposting is not the main activity that transforms organic waste into humus, pure consumption is. Worms are voracious eaters and consume most of the organic kitchen scraps produced in the kitchen. Although worms may naturally consume decaying animals when clearing off a forest floor, you do not want to feed our indoor worms meat products due to the risks of odors and pathogenic bacteria growth. Similarly, you do not want to deposit dairy products into our worm bins.

Worm Menu

Foods that can be fed on a regular basis:

Apples	Carrots	Pears
Avocados	Cereal	Potatoes
Bananas	Corn	Squash
Banana peels	Eggplant	Spinach
Bell peppers	Grapes	Tomatoes
Berries	Lettuce	Watermelon
Broccoli	Mangos	Zucchini
Cantaloupe	Peaches	

Foods easily eaten by worms but diet shouldn't be limited to these:

Breads (minimal)	Egg cartons, wet	Paper towels
Coffee grounds	Egg shells, crushed	Rice
Cardboard (plain)	Leaves, dried	Tea bags
Copy paper, shredded	Muffins	Tea leaves
Dryer lint (no dryer sheets)	Newspaper	Tissues, clean
	Oatmeal	

Worms don't like these foods. They have preferences and may leave some of the below items to rot and create odor in the bin:

Butter	Green grass & yard waste	Oils
Citrus, large amounts		Onions
Dairy	Hot peppers	Spicy & pickled foods
Garlic	Leeks	Vinegar
Glossy paper	Meat	

Like outdoor composting, there is a team of workers/consumers in a worm bin. The worms are the most obvious, but microorganisms are also essential to help break down food scraps prior to consumption by the worms. Unlike the various temperature-based bacteria that heat up an outdoor bin, the bacteria in a worm bin thrive in more moderate temperatures. Heat is not necessary in this efficient form of indoor composting. A worm bin requires temperatures between 40° F and 85° F (4° C–29° C) to survive and thrives at room temperature within the range of 60° F and 75° F (16° C–24° C), the perfect indoor requirement no matter where you live.

The number and type of worms housed makes all the difference when vermicomposting. There are several thousand species of worms on the planet, but the red wiggler is the best worm for an in-home worm composting system. When starting a bin, be sure to purchase red wigglers to ensure success. Worms can be purchased from online sources or locally at bait shops, but bait shops frequently sell them by the dozen. Although these little guys reproduce quickly, a dozen will not be sufficient to process the quantity of kitchen scraps produced by a typical household. A starter batch of a thousand working worms is the minimum for most new worm bins. Composting worms can consume approximately one half of their body weight a day. Therefore, a pound of worms, approximately a thousand will consume a half-pound of waste per day. In my experience as a vermicomposting educator, a pound of working worms is sufficient for most individuals. A family of two, or three, people will need to start with a larger population, two to three thousand worms.

As we will discuss further in chapter 7, worms reproduce quickly, but some new composters become frustrated waiting for their worms to reproduce. When people finally decide to commit to a worm bin or composting effort, they often are a bit impatient. They blame the process for being slow or the worms for being lazy if they cannot manage the waste stream adequately. I like to remind my clients that their waste stream, not the quantity of worms, is the starting point. All they really need to do is get the right amount of staff for the workload. More worms equals more waste consumed!

There are many commercially manufactured worm bins available online in addition to guidelines on how to build your own. The size and shape of the structure necessary to house your new roommates is based on the amount of waste you expect to feed the worms. Since composting worms naturally live on the surface of the planet, a deep bin structure such as a garbage can, is not recommended. A wider and shallow apparatus with more surface area is the way to go. In her book *Worms Eat My Garbage,* Mary Appelhof recommends that you plan on one square foot of surface for each pound of garbage per week that you plan to feed your worms.[1]

In addition to the pounds of waste per week that you accumulate, accounting for a few more details will help you determine the best size worm bin to purchase and the amount of worms you will need. Do you eat out often? Are you a vegetarian? Does your family grow a lot of fresh fruits and vegetables? How often are you throwing away leftovers?

1. Mary Appelhof, *Worms Eat My Garbage,* 2d ed. (Kalamazoo: FlowerPress, 1997).

What to Do With the Pit?

The next time you finish making guacamole, don't throw away that pit! Bury it in your worm bin. No, the worms won't be able to eat it, but the nutrient-rich environment will sprout this giant seed in no time at all. In the old days, my mother used to struggle to insert toothpicks into these avocado pits and balance them in just the right amount of water waiting for them to sprout. Though this may eventually happen, no need to struggle with those old methods. Just let the nutrients and moisture in the worm bin do their job and you will have a taproot sprouting out of the bottom of the pit within about a month. Once you see this root, take the pit out and plant it in a pot to continue growing. Sprinkle on some more worm casting when you plant it and it will continue to thrive in your home or on your back porch. Try this with a mango pit, too.

Our lifestyles are very closely linked to our waste stream. As we explore composting methods in general, we have a clearer view into our life habits. When I am working long hours, I eat out much more frequently and my worm food consists mainly of coffee grounds, tea bags, and apple cores. As my summer schedule shifts to working outdoor farmers' markets, I have beautiful leftover greens, peaches, and mushroom stems for my worms. In the heart of the winter months, my worms are thriving on soup stock, vegetable peelings, celery stalks, leftover rice, bread crusts, and those same old coffee grounds and tea bags. When I am in need of comfort food, I am aware that the pizza cardboard will be the added fiber source for the worms that night.

On more than one occasion, worm clients of mine have commented that once they started housing and feeding worms, they became much more aware of their own diets and choices. This may very well be another way to clean up our diets and embark on more mindful living. Worms don't care for corndogs and pizza, but boy do they love cantaloupe, berries, and greens! You should take note of this you we plan your daily meals. Keeping the worms happy may in turn keep you healthy.

Indoor composting is accessible to all. The skills and space needed to start are minimal. Yet, because vermicomposting requires a commitment to thousands of living beings on the planet, it is important to learn a bit more about their needs and preferences. Housing creatures of any sort requires this added effort. You need to understand the temperament, dietary concerns, activity levels, and lifespan of your composting worms. As Urban Worm Girl, I have taken it upon myself to really get to know my

"Don't worry, they know what to do, just give them a good home and watch."

worms over the years, and I have made a sincere effort to pass this on to all who want to listen. As I educate and install worm bins, I help people get to know their red wigglers, teaching them skills of observation as well as facts. I distinctly remember the day my first batch of wigglers arrived in the mail. I did not have a local contact to meet with for a formal introduction or for hand-holding. I was so nervous, questioning, and doubtful of my ability to care for these beings. Having fifteen years experience in healthcare prepared me for many things, but not caring for worms! The only thing I could think to do at the time was call my friend in Berkeley for support. I distinctly remember her words and pass them on to my clients regularly. In response to my fears of killing the worms, she calmly said, "Don't worry, they know what to do. Just give them a good home and watch." Wow, that made sense. These creatures were given instincts to survive and have done so for thousands of years despite their fragile structures. I just needed to give them a good home and watch. So that is what I did and what I will outline a bit further for you.

7: Worms and Our Soil

"It may be doubted whether there are many other animals which have played so important a part in the history of the world, as have these lowly organized creatures."

—Charles Darwin

Healthy soil is often referred to as loam. It is soil with just the right texture, structure, and viability. This loam contains all the necessary attributes to sustain life. It is porous enough to allow water to percolate through to plant roots housed at varying levels within. All the while, its balanced composition of silt, sand, clay, and organic matter retains some of this moisture at the surface level much like a sponge. This saves resources for future use—how smart!

This loamy texture also allows air and nutrients to move freely, nourishing plants and the soil creatures tending to them. As we have seen in previous chapters, healthy soil is not a given. Soil sometimes needs our help to create this loamy texture. Much like adding spinach to our plate to create a balanced meal, we can alter the ingredients of our soil to modify its makeup and increase its overall health. Guess who can help us to do this in the most efficient way? That's correct: worms! Though he was most well know for his theories of evolution and natural selection, Charles Darwin spent the last thirty years of his life studying how these amazing little creatures care for our soil.

Like that fresh, green, leafy vegetable on the dinner plate helps to feed our bodies, composting enables us to put nutrients and organic matter back into nutrient-deprived, dry soil. This addition not only feeds the soil, it alters its composition. There is no more direct way to do this than by recruiting hard-working worms. Worms are the natural experts in this area. Composting with worms, within the home mimics the role that worms naturally play in recycling nutrients and building healthy soil particles. This simple and odorless form of composting can be done almost anywhere once you recruit the worms. A worm bin is especially well suited for smaller homes, condos, and apartments because it requires little space. Created within such a small space, the product, known as vermicompost, packs a big punch. The benefits of adding vermicompost to the soil are tremendous. And don't be fooled, a little goes a long way.

Aristotle referred to worms as the intestines of the earth. What a perfect description of these spineless creatures who wriggle, writhe, burrow, aerate, chew, digest, process, till, transform, and eventually excrete organic matter across the surface of the planet. How can such small spineless creatures do such heavy work? They are actually built for the job. Worms exist in almost all regions of the earth. There are over four thousand identified species and many more still unfamiliar to us. The diversity among these species is amazing and yet most of us may just assume a worm is a worm, some big, some small. Worms are found in lakes, streams, mountains, plains, gardens, and forests. Soil-dwelling worms, earthworms, are the most well known due to their

Real People, Real Worms:
The Adventures of the Urban Worm Girl

As Urban Worm Girl, I educate the public about the wisdom of the red wiggler composting worm. I also sell worms by the pound and all the necessary worm bin equipment. Selling worms often feels like trafficking illegal substances. Weighing out the product, bagging it up, and packing it in a nondescript bag for delivery seems questionable, even to me, at times. I have a scale in my kitchen and take orders by the pound over the phone and via e-mail. I pride myself in meeting my clients and providing personalized assistance. Therefore, I often make "the drop" where it will be convenient for my clients and in a way that minimizes the need for a third party, such as the postal service. Starbucks parking lots, city parks during kids' baseball games, grocery stores on a Sunday afternoon, or the front or back porch of someone's home has often been the scene of the "crime." In the beginning, I was nervous to show up at a stranger's house or in a random suburban parking lot, but now I treasure these unique moments. Who will be on the other end of the deal? Usually it's a very interesting individual with whom I share a very specific common interest: *worms*! How often do you get to say that? Here are some of my favorite worm encounters. Not only are these initial meetings fascinating, but the follow-up calls can also be full of surprises.

- Sunday afternoon at the Starbucks parking lot: I had the name of a husband who was to pick up a worm bin and pound of worms between soccer games. I arrived a bit early and decided to pop over to the grocery store. On my way back to the meeting, I saw a young man and a child in soccer clothes. We made eye contact and I nodded. He immediately smiled a nervous smile and walked towards my car to finish the deal. We worm people can just sense each other I guess?

- After the initial phone call, the details were laid out with Phil. We had agreed upon a one-pound drop at his house on Friday afternoon. He was going to be out for the day but requested that the drop be made in the backyard. This was a first for me. He was to leave a check under the lid of the BBQ and I was to take it and exchange it for the worms. It felt weird to leave my treasured worms under the lid of a BBQ, yet I did just that and all is well to this day.

- A young couple I met, much to even my surprise, decided to keep their homemade worm bin under their bed. It was a great conversation piece at cocktail parties when asked how they had room to compost in a studio apartment.

- Another young couple had a similarly small apartment, a large dog, and the husband's full drum set. It was obvious that they were determined to compost when they decided to place the worm bin on top of the dog crate in the corner. Now this is dedication!

- One of my favorite stories as a worm girl and compost educator is the story of a young man who was adding a worm bin to his one bedroom, third floor apartment that he was soon to share with his girlfriend. As we were determining the best place to keep his bin, he eliminated the far northeast corner of the apartment because, as he said, "This is where my girlfriend will be keeping her rats." He went on to say that, "Rats really get a bad rap, but my girlfriend is part of a rat rescue program in Chicago and we have cages set for that corner." I of course responded, "Yeah, I understand, worms get a pretty bad rap as well." We chose another corner for the worms.
- I recently delivered three pounds of worms to an artist in Chicago who was going to incorporate the worms into an environmental art installation for a local university. I was overjoyed about the fact that my worms were not only going to be famous but they were going to continue educating the masses about their wisdom as composters and earth workers.
- A story that has always amazed and inspired me is of a couple with added challenges in caring for a worm bin and its thousand inhabitants. They were obviously committed to maintaining a home worm bin and were successfully doing so in spite of the fact that the wife is wheelchair-bound and her husband is blind.
- Elaine so kindly called out of genuine concern for the health of her worms. She was definitely beating around the bush about her main area of concern, but she eventually revealed she was worried that her worms—all thousand plus of them—were constipated. I took her concerns seriously, but as she began to describe her reasons for concern, I realized that she was basing her worry on the swollen area of their body most closely related to reproduction. She was sure that this swelling was indicative of a digestive impairment. I appreciated her observation skills as well as her general compassion for other beings, but I had to laugh. "Elaine, they are fertile, not blocked up!" She laughed a hearty belly laugh and said, "Oh! Thanks, have a good night" and hung up. I love putting clients at ease, so I hung up and went to bed with a renewed sense of purpose. I love my job.

home of choice. Yet earthworms are not all the same either, far from it. All terrestrial, earthbound worms provide assistance to the soil. Each has varied characteristics that suits it for its particular climate and environment. A worm is not just a worm!

TYPES OF EARTHBOUND WORMS

Most earthworms are not native to the United States. The family of earthworms that is most important in enhancing agricultural soil is *Lumbricidae*, which originated in Europe and have been transported by human activities to many parts of the world. It is believed that many earthworms were actually transported in potted plants across the ocean to the New World. Though earthworms are indigenous to Europe, they are now common in all parts of the world except extreme climate zones, polar, and arid areas. Earthworm populations tend to increase with higher levels of soil organic matter and decrease with soil disturbances, such as tillage and potentially harmful chemicals.[1] In good soil, there are up to fifty earthworms in a square foot.[2]

There are three major categories of these earthworms that live in the soil: *endogeic, anecic* and *epigeic.* The types are defined by the level of the earth in which they reside and the surface leaf litter they prefer—the often rich layer of topsoil or the lower levels of subsoil full of minerals. Not all of these worms are built to be part of your com-

Worm Fact: Worms are made up of 75–90 percent water! Keeping their skin moist is essential to their health because worms breathe through their skins.

posting team. Though all worms will eat organic matter, some species will not be happy or remain healthy in the enclosed environment necessary for worm-bin composting. I don't recommend that you go out back after reading this book and dig up some of your native worms to get your worm

1. Clive A. Edwards, "Soil Biology Primer Chapter 8: Earthworms," USDA Natural Resource Conservation Services, http://soils.usda.gov/sqi/concepts/soil_biology/earthworms.html (accessed May 5, 2010).

2. Jeff Lowenfels and Wayne Lewis. *Teaming with Microbes: A Gardener's Guide to the Soil Food Web* (Portland: Timber Press, 2006).

bin started. It's not likely that you would end up with the right worm for the job that you have defined. In some instances, you might even end up with a mess and a few escapees! It's important to understand some differences within the worm population when committing vermicomposting.

You may want to think of the majority of the worms you find in your garden as "earthworkers" versus "composters." Earthworkers are the worms that move the soil, burrow, and aerate. They are working and preparing the soil for future growing. Of course, they are eating and excreting worm castings along the way, but they are not primarily performing composting skills. In contrast, the surface dwelling worm, such as the red wiggler, is a "composter," eating its way across the surface of the planet, and it is perfect for a worm bin. But let's review a bit about each of the varieties (endogeic, anecic, and epigeic earthworms) to best understand why the red wiggler is so well suited for your worm bin.

Endogeic Worms

Commonly called field or gray worms, endogeic worms are grayish-pink in color and rarely come to the surface. Instead, they inhabit the deeper mineral layers of the earth. *Endo* literally means "within" in Latin. They prefer to reside in the soil, around the roots of plants, or deep under logs.[3] Although these worms consume more soil than other worms, they reproduce slowly and less frequently. They live deep in the earth working the soil and creating permanent burrows. They do not surface to consume the varied contents of debris on the top layer of the earth. They are not well suited for a compost bin, which relies on shallow depth and will contain a significant variety of organic matter for consumption.

Anecic Worms

The nightcrawler, a member of the *Lumbricidae* family, is the best-known type of anecic worm and the one you probably see most frequently in the garden. These creatures build permanent burrows in the soil but often rise to the surface. Their favorite time to surface tends to be at night. During the day, they retreat underground, pulling leaves and other organic matter into their burrows that can extend several meters into the

3. Amy Stewart, "Worms' Work," *Organic Gardening*, April/May 2004, 52–54.

soil. Though they peruse the surface debris, they do not actually remain on the surface to eat. Darwin confirmed this in his years of research as he tracked the movement of small leaves from one location to another by means of earthworm transport. This is an important fact when considering what type of worm to keep in an enclosed environment within your home. You want to house a breed of worms that are happy to live and eat in one location. You do not want to house nightcrawlers for this job due to their traveling tendencies.

Nightcrawlers are sturdy, strong members of the species. They can easily live for five to six years and are about six inches long, easily stretching to 10" or 12" (25cm–30cm) when in motion. Their flattened, spoon-shaped tail and thick meaty build makes them easy to recognize.[4] They are frequently found in backyard gardens and are a sign of healthy soil. They have the ability to burrow into the ground to depths of at least 6' (2m), performing the important job of mixing the soil as they travel. The tunnels created during their deep burrowing allow air and water to reach the root systems of many plants, and they provide sanctuaries for their individual winter hibernation. Surviving a cold winter is not a problem when skilled at achieving this burrowing depth. The surface of the earth may freeze, but these worms can burrow deep enough underground to survive even the cold winters of the Midwest. The nightcrawler, though a uniquely skilled "earthworker" and essential for soil health, is not the best worm to employ in your worm bin.

Epigeic Worms

The most common compost worm is an epigeic worm. In Latin, *epi* means "on" or "upon" and *geic* refers to the Earth itself. The surface of the Earth is the preferred environment for this type of worm. The most common epigeic worm in the United States is the red wiggler, also known in Latin as *Eisenia fetida*. The red wiggler thrives in the top 6"–12" (15cm–30cm) of the soil, feeding on large amounts of dead and decaying organic matter, transforming it into new soil. This is what they are born to do, and they are, therefore, physically built for this task of consumption. Luckily, they also like to eat "locally," where the food is. They don't feel the need to waste

4. Amy Stewart, "Worms' Work," *Organic Gardening*, April/May 2004, 52– 54.

Eisenia fetida more commonly know as the red wiggler are excellent composting worms.

time by transporting their food to another area before dining. Where they live is where they eat. These creatures don't survive long in ordinary garden soil alone. There is not enough organic matter there for them to feed on. They prefer compost piles and layers of thick mulch, where they feed off rotting organic matter. Red wigglers have a life span of about two to three years, but reproduce regularly when the conditions support the growth of a new population.[5] Though they are surprisingly small when compared to their larger cousins, the nightcrawlers, they consume debris at an alarming rate. They are hearty, adaptable, and have the ability to survive within fluctuating pH soil levels, making them particularly well-suited for the varied conditions within a worm bin.

These are the worms that are recommended for an in-home worm composting bin. They eat, poop, and reproduce on a regular basis, just the skill set we need to be successful when vermicomposting. Staying local while eating voraciously, red wigglers will consume at least half their body weight each day in food. When healthy, they reproduce regularly keeping a full workforce employed at all times. They are small and kind of cute, too. Really, they are. I was so relieved to find out that I did not have to house big, fat nightcrawlers in my home to compost with worms. Red wigglers are small, reddish worms with a yellowish color on the tip of their tail.

5. Ibid.

RED WIGGLERS INSIDE AND OUT

Understanding a bit more about worms will help you properly care for a full workforce of red wigglers in your composting efforts. These top-feeding, hearty worms are made up of ringed segments. The red wiggler is specifically composed of eighty to 120 segments created by circular muscles running the length of the creature. When contracting and expanding, these muscles propel the worm through its environment. Though a worm appears smooth and limbless, it actually has small bristles extending out from each segment that serve a purpose similar to limbs. The *setae*, or bristles, along each segment of the worm help to steer and stabilize it for efficient locomotion. When threatened by a local predator, such as a hungry robin, these setae also hold on to the surrounding soil to defend against attack. These hair-like protrusions are amazingly strong. If you reach into your bin and grab a single worm, you can feel the pullback of the tiny creature between your fingers. This is a simple way to feel the setae function without causing harm. The next time the sun comes out after a rain, watch the robins fighting for their meals (the local worm populations). Though the birds are larger and appear stronger, they don't always win the fight.

In addition to their ability to fend off predators with their setae, the red wiggler has another unique defense mechanism. The Latin name, *fetida* literally means "to stink." These wigglers have the ability to release a yellowish, foul-smelling fluid from their tail end when threatened. Hence the reference to "stink" in their name. Though harmless to humans, this fluid is noxious to a bird or mole who may attempt to snack on one of these worms. The yellowish coloring on the tip of the red wiggler tail is one distinguishing characteristic of this particular variety. It is an easy way to be assured that you indeed have received red wigglers when purchasing your worms.

The worm's skin, which in the case of our red wiggler, is reddish in color, is one of its most vital organs. The entire outer covering functions like our lungs, breathing in the air needed for survival. Worms have no lungs. Although worms need air to live, they also require moisture for the process of respiration to occur. A dry environment limits respiration and can quickly kill a worm. In just three minutes of direct sunlight, a worm will dehydrate and die.[6] We have all witnessed this tragedy along our paved sidewalks where worms are unable to find shade or a patch of grass to burrow into. After the rain and clouds pass and the sun reappears, the worms are left vulnerable on the steamy concrete. Similarly, excess moisture may drown a worm. Remember, these are soil-dwelling worms. The familiar tragic scene involving dried worms scattered across the sidewalk starts with a storm and the need for the worms to evacuate to higher ground to prevent drowning in the water-soaked ground. Proper levels of moisture play a key role in worm survival and will be an important factor for an overall healthy worm bin.

Worms have five valved chambers that pump blood throughout their body. These chambers could be considered their hearts. Unlike a human circulatory system, these hearts also pump urine for excretion through the skin. In addition to breathing through their skin, worms actually excrete urine through their skin.

Most importantly, red wiggler worms are master composters, consuming at least half of their body weight a day, and yet they have no teeth and very small mouths. Unlike humans, a worm's process of digestion does not start off in the mouth by chewing and breaking down food.

6. Shelley C. Grossman and Toby Weitzel. *Recycle With Earthworms: The Red Wiggler Connection* (Eagle River: Shields Press, 1997).

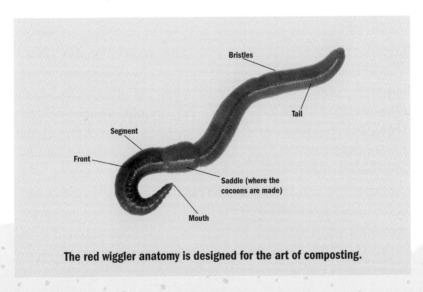

Bristles

Tail

Segment

Front

Saddle (where the cocoons are made)

Mouth

The red wiggler anatomy is designed for the art of composting.

The worms are dependent on helpers in the surrounding environment to soften and prepare large pieces of organic matter for consumption. The process of chewing starts outside of the worm in the ecosystem of surrounding microorganisms. Once the soil team of molds, fungi, bacteria and bugs predigest organic matter, the worms locate these now much smaller particles with special sensory organs within their mouths. Believe it or not, in addition to having no teeth, the worms have no eyes to see their meals. They keenly sense their food with these specially adapted organs. Once located, they then process the food waste further within their bodies. This process of predigesting occurring outside of the worms is especially relevant for these toothless creatures.

In addition to lacking teeth and eyes, worms have no ears and no nose. They receive all of their sensory input through vibration, heat, light, and moisture levels. Remarkable! Once they locate a food source, they are able to suction the matter into their mouth and further down into

Worms have no teeth, no eyes, no ears and no nose. They receive all of their sensory input through vibration, heat, light, and moisture levels.

the esophagus until it reaches the gizzard. Like chickens, worms pulverize food within a gizzard. Your crushed eggshells, when added to the bin, will help mimic the role of teeth. Like sand and grit in natural soils, worms use these coarse substances to further chew the organic matter they ingest within their gizzard.

Possibly the most fascinating and impressive part of a worm's anatomy is the colony of microorganisms living and working within the gastrointestinal tract. Bacteria, fungi, protozoa, and enzymes not only assist with digestion, but later, when excreted as castings in the compost, they provide the plants with nutrients. Some of the specific enzymes unique to worms act as antibiotics and insecticides that keep the worms, and later the plants, free from harm. I believe that these enzymes also protect us as we handle worm waste in our worm bins. Once again, do not fear the miniature world of bacteria; praise their efforts.

Reproduction is essential in a worm bin if there is hope to maintain its productivity and output over a long period of time. Most earthworms, including the red wigglers, are hermaphrodites—they have both sets of sexual organs. They mate by lining up, head-to-tail, and producing sticky mucus that holds them together during what might otherwise be very slippery business.[7] In addition to the binding agent of the mucus, the worms actually hold onto each other with those small, bristle-like setae. After exchanging the necessary secretions to fertilize one another, the couple wriggles free from the embrace to form individual cocoons to be deposited in the surrounding soil. Each participant forms a cocoon, doubling the traditional potential for offspring. The resulting caramel-colored cocoons are quite small and resemble a seed or a tiny lemon. The makeup of the cocoon contains all the nutrients needed by the developing hatchlings held inside. The entire process can take about three hours and can result in three to five hatchlings from each cocoon. I have to admit that this worm mating ritual is completely fascinating to me. Sometimes I have felt like a voyeur when coming across an entwined worm couple at the top of my bin. At times, I have lingered long enough to snap a photo or two to mark the moment in time forever.

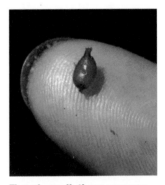

Though small, these cocoons may hold 3 to 5 hatchlings.

The presence of numerous cocoons is an indication of a happy and healthy worm population and balanced environment. When conditions are less than desirable to support young hatchlings, the cocoons will lay dormant for up to three years—another amazing characteristic of the red wiggler worm that enhances its survival rate and ability to be successfully housed in a worm bin.

The more worms housed in a bin, the more efficient the worm bin is. That means that the more worms you have, the more garbage and food waste they will process. Some people think that they can increase the worm population by cutting worms in two and creating two worms. In fact, although a worm with its tail cut off can usually grow a new one, a severed tail will not grow a new head. A much easier (and more effective)

7. Amy Stewart, "Worms' Work," *Organic Gardening*, April/May 2004, 52–54.

way to help your worms increase and multiply is to support their environment.[8] Build a safe and balanced home for your worms and they will serve you well and reproduce on a consistent basis.

WORM CASTINGS: THE BLACK GOLD OF VERMICULTURE

Composting with worms does not only minimize your waste stream, it gives you a beautiful and valuable product in the process. Worm castings (also known as worm poop) are extremely high in nutrients needed by the soil and plant life as well as high in organic matter (humus). Worm castings contain 40 to 50 percent more humus than the average top layer of soil. Earthworms speed the decomposition of dead plant roots, manure, and other organic matter, such as leaf litter and animal carcasses. They reduce soil compaction as they burrow and swallow soil. After swallowing the soil, the worm transports it and deposits it in a new location, moving nutrients to a new location as well. Their casts create tiny clumps of soil that hold in nutrients and resist erosion. Though these red wiggler worms may be small, they work hard to process the debris on the surface of the earth and in worm bins. In nature, they can leave behind ten to fifteen tons of castings per acre each year.[9]

Worms introduce a rich, diverse community of microorganisms into the soil through their waste. The beneficial bacteria inside of a worm's gut digest organic material and create castings. Castings are coated with polysaccharide, simple proteins, and carbohydrates, which help support the external bacterial population. The bacteria and microorganisms, in turn, support plant life and interact with and nourish other creatures in the soil web. It's a very sustainable model that Mother Nature has created for our learning! Each creature is designed to support each other as well as the bigger picture.

The bacteria within a worm's digestive track specifically release stored nutrients from their food so it is in the perfect form for plant absorption. Research shows that when earthworms consume nutrients like calcium, those nutrients are converted into a form that is easier for plants to use.[10]

8. Ibid.

9. Jeff Lowenfels and Wayne Lewis. *Teaming with Microbes: A Gardener's Guide to the Soil Food Web* (Portland: Timber Press, 2006).

Through this process, worm castings offer up phosphate, potash, nitrogen, magnesium, and calcium at rates much higher than found in soil without worms. When compared to soil without worms, soil with worms can contain as much as:

- seven times the phosphate
- ten times the potash
- five times the nitrogen
- three times the magnesium
- 1.5 times the calcium

Some chemical fertilizers and soil amendments may indeed add the same nutrients to your soil, but they are not adding organic matter in the form of humus and microorganisms, which are essential components in soil. Adding compost and, in particular, vermicompost to your soil adds all the necessary components for both plant and soil life. Worms are naturally doing this when they are present. All gardeners would agree that the presence of earthworms when preparing for planting is a good sign.

The makeup of all compost varies a great deal based on the organic matter being processed. The resulting soil-like substance can contain different levels of nitrogen and phosphorus or it can vary in the makeup of its microorganisms. Some compost results in a bacterial dominant product and some is fungal dominant. Remember, these microorganisms are all beneficial to the soil health, but some plants prefer one over another. Because vermicompost is distinctly bacterially dominant, it is an excellent amendment for veggie and flower gardening as well as for lawn fertilizing. Fungal-dominant compost, usually the product of nonworm compost, is best for use on trees, shrubs, and perennials.[11] Learning what specific garden plants prefer is a level of master gardening that can be explored further in gardening books and workshops. Check with your local extension office for a list of resources.

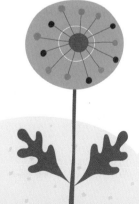

10. Amy Stewart, "Worms' Work," *Organic Gardening*, April/May 2004, 52–54.

11. Jeff Lowenfels and Wayne Lewis. *Teaming with Microbes: A Gardener's Guide to the Soil Food Web* (Portland: Timber Press, 2006).

In residential-scale vermicomposting, heating up of organic matter is minimal if present at all. Worms are ingesting your waste prior to full decomposition from thermophilic (hot) bacteria. You don't want a bacterially hot environment for this type of composting. Not only does heat kill off some of the diversity of microorganisms, it can also harm the worms. If the compost reaches hot-pile temperatures—145° F to 150° F (63° C–66° C)—for any length of time, the worms will head elsewhere. If they have nowhere to go, they will die. In addition, heat is not essential to control the bad guys (weeds and pathogens) in a vermicompost. The worms themselves do much of the work on the enemy lines. They ingest the root-feeding nematodes, the pathogenic bacteria and fungi, and the small-sized weed seeds. What they don't convert fully gets released from their digestive system as fecal material (castings) and the pathogens, root-feeding nematodes, and weed seed usually don't survive the complex digestive processes. The conditions in vermicompost are not right for the bad guys and they die, or barely survive at best.[12] Warning: The seeds that are too large for the worms to ingest, such as cantaloupe or squash seeds, may actually begin to grow within the nutrient-rich environment of your worm bin.

Worms ingest the root-feeding nematodes, the pathogenic bacteria and fungi, and the small-sized weed seeds. What they don't convert fully gets released from their digestive system as fecal material (castings).

HOUSING WORMS

The benefits of employing a working population becomes clear as you explore the natural role of worms and the magic of their excrement on the planet. They can simultaneously reduce your waste stream by eating your kitchen and paper scraps while creating a valuable soil amendment. Worms are very efficient at transforming large amounts of waste into manageable amounts of black gold. Their resulting output is reduced by

12. Elaine Ingham, "Is Vermicompost Better than Compost?" *Tilth Producers Quarterly*, Spring 1999.

approximately 50 to 60 percent in volume, so you will not be at risk of overflowing in worm castings, even if you do not have a garden or yard to use them in immediately. Storing the valuable product or giving it away is completely feasible.

How exactly do you start? If you are on a budget or you enjoy do-it-yourself projects, you may choose to build your own worm bin. Chapter 8 will give you specific guidelines on how to do this with a basic plastic tub purchased at the local hardware or home store.

8: Getting Started With Worms

"What would our lives be like if we took the earthworms seriously, took the ground under our feet rather than the skies high above our heads, as the place to be? It is as though we have been pointed in the wrong direction."

—From *Darwin's Worms* by Adam Phillips

So you decided to take the plunge and host a thousand worms. Over the years, I've used many different apparatus to house my worm populations. I try to pass on all that I have learned to my customers and fit them with the best "worm condo" for their particular lifestyle. Returning from Berkeley, California (where I first met the worms), I scoured the Internet in search of worm bins. Like many, I was drawn to the lower-cost options due to my budget and uncertainty about my commitment to such a new process. I wasn't quite ready to make a financial commitment to my worm composting efforts. What if I failed? What if the worms didn't like me?

I ordered a simple low-cost worm farm off an Internet site. It was guaranteed to make my vermicomposting efforts succeed, and it included starter bedding and a pound of red wiggler worms for a reasonable fee. I was sorely disappointed when it arrived. I had actually paid for a Rubbermaid tub with a couple of holes drilled in it. I could have easily made this for a quarter of the cost, especially when considering the added cost of shipping. If my memory serves me correctly, this "special worm farm" was shipped all the way from Pennsylvania to Chicago. Luckily the worms were healthy and are still living to this day, or at least their offspring are. If you are starting fresh with little experience, beware of any offer that does not include a picture of the product. Know what you are ordering so that you are not surprised. Low-cost options are definitely possible, but not all products for sale on the Internet are worth their cost.

DIY VS. COMMERCIAL WORM BINS

If you are on a budget or you enjoy do-it-yourself projects, you may choose to build your own worm bin. I will give you specific guidelines on how to do this for little expense with a basic tub purchased at the local hardware or home store (see page 140). If you prefer the most convenient and efficient approach to new projects, I recommend exploring the upward migration system. Either method is extremely effective for housing worms and creating black gold, yet one may better fit your lifestyle. In my experience, individuals have more success with the care and maintenance of upward migration systems because the design itself helps to keep the bin cleaner and, therefore, the worms a bit healthier.

Because this migration system utilizes the natural instinctual behavior of red wiggler worms as surface dwellers, a form of self-separation takes place. Worms seek out food and scraps towards the upper surfaces of the trays. Additionally, worms move away from their waste, leaving it behind for you to easily remove. The grated stacking trays of this migration system were developed to encourage the worms to move upwards towards the new food source and leave their castings behind for easy harvest.

Less time and handling of worms and worm castings means more frequent harvests and less chance for excessive buildup of contaminants and moisture. Even though worms do ingest their own waste several times, (refining its texture each time), castings eventually become toxic to the worms and a fresh environment is needed. Simply adding on a new tray of bedding and food scraps easily accomplishes this. Two or three trays are sufficient to manage between five and eight thousand worms and the majority of one household's waste.

Another consideration is size and appearance. A worm bin functions based on the surface area available for the worms and materials to occupy. Depth is not the primary need, therefore a garbage can, though it has a greater volume and does not have a large footprint, will not work well as a commercial worm bin. Surface-dwelling worms need to stay within the first 8" to 12" (20cm–30cm) of any container. The DIY bin requires a 10-gallon (38 Liter) tote to house at least 1 to 2 pounds (.5kg–1kg) of worms, the amount of worms necessary to handle the waste of a one or two person household. The surface area within this 10-gallon tote will allow for several thousand worms to live and consume waste. A larger, homemade bin will need to have a larger footprint if it is not stackable. Though this is not a large apparatus, its footprint is a bit larger than some of the commercial upward migration bins. Because of the additional stackable trays, a migration bin has increased surface area and can therefore house more working worms. More worms means more efficient food waste consumption.

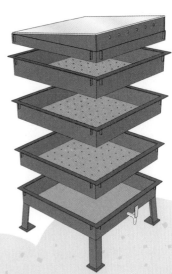

Compared to the single-space tote (above), an upward-migration bin (right) maximizes working worm space, increases castings yield, and makes the whole process much easier to manage.

Depending on where you are planning on keeping your worm bin, the appearance may be a concern. The commercial bins have a simple and compact design and can be purchased in black or green. The bin that I prefer has a sloped roof and has a slight Asian feel. I call it the worm pagoda and think it is quite attractive. Mine is housed in my kitchen and fits right in next to the counter. Some may not be as comfortable leaving a large storage tote exposed in the kitchen. If appearance is important to you, explore the commercial migration bins.

 Two or three trays are sufficient to manage between five to eight thousand worms and the majority of one household's waste.

It is recommended that a worm bin be kept in a convenient location where you will be able to easily access it. It is also important to take temperatures into consideration because the worms need moderate temperatures to stay alive and hungry. Remember that worms thrive within a temperature range of 60° F–75° F (16° C–24° C), eating voraciously and reproducing frequently. They will perish if temperatures dip below freezing or soar above 85° F–90° F (29° C–32° C). Most home interiors stay within this temperature range because humans also thrive within these temperature ranges. If your plan is to keep your bin in a garage or on an outdoor porch, be aware of the temperature requirements of the worms.

The most common places to keep worm bins are in the basement, the laundry room, a storage closet, the kitchen pantry, under the kitchen sink, or in the second bathroom. I have met individuals that keep their worms in the bedroom or in the living room as well. There is no rule here and because odor is not an issue, your guests won't mind. Frankly, they may not even know you are housing thousands of worms. If you choose to keep your worms in the garage, make sure to insulate the bin in the winter and watch for steamy temperatures in the summer. You may need to bring it inside for best results.

MIGRATION BINS

There are several brands of commercial migration bins available. They all operate based on the same principles. They vary a bit in size, shape, and color but are generally plastic. Many are made of a high percentage of post-consumer recycled plastic but not 100 percent because at that percentage, the plastic can become very brittle and break with frequent use. The design is more complicated than a single tub bin and consists of more parts and assembly and, therefore, is a bit more costly.

After about six months of using my homemade worm bin, I realized why these expensive options existed for housing worms. Time and space is required to maintain and harvest a single tub-type worm bin, such as the mail-order worm farm I began with or the DIY bin. The worms and the food are constantly intermingled making it hard to separate and remove the castings while leaving the worms behind to keep working. Over time, the contents become even more compacted as castings accumulate and the separation becomes even more challenging. Not to mention, it can be a dirty job. There is often a necessity for getting your hands deep down in the contents of the bin and hand-separating the stubborn worms from their resulting castings. Many individuals, though invested in composting, have a difficult time handling the worms and their waste. This is a reality that may shift over time, but it is important to consider in the beginning. There are methods to simplify "harvesting" in a single tub system, making the process as efficient as possible. (This is discussed further on page 144.) However, the fact remains, that there is one large space for the worms, their food, and their waste to share.

Photo Courtesy of Gusanito Worm Bins

Time constraints are a concern for many like myself. The upward migration bin is designed to encourage instinctual behavior in the worms. Red wiggler worms are surface dwellers and an upward migration design uses this instinct to move towards the surface. As new food is added in a new tray above, the worms move towards it on their own accord, lessening the work needed to separate worms from finished compost (vermicastings). Worms move from lower trays to upper trays through grated openings in search of these new layers of bedding and food. As worms finish their meals in the lower trays and move upward, the lower trays are ready for harvesting. The worms have left their casting behind in search of sweeter pastures, making your job easier.

Preparing a Migration Bin

A migration system consists of three to five, low-profile, square or round identical trays, depending on the brand. As mentioned earlier, red wiggler composting worms are surface dwellers and will not thrive in a deep and compacted environment. The depth of each tray is approximately 8" (20cm) which, accurately simulates the top surface of the earth. Each open tray is grated on the bottom surface to allow movement between the layers. The initial phase of composting will start with only one tray and the roof. You can store the remaining trays for use in about two months.

Most systems also have a liquid collection tray within the base to allow liquid leachate to flow freely through and separate the worms from the dangers of drowning. In addition, the flow-through structure minimizes excessive moisture. This feature also keeps pathogenic bacteria from building up and creating an odor. It can be helpful to add a porous fabric between the lower grated tray and the liquid collection tray to keep the worms from dropping through to the liquid below. The Urban Worm Girl system comes with a fabric barrier cloth to serve this purpose. If needed, you can purchase a porous weed barrier fabric at a hardware store and cut it to fit your system of choice.

Prior to stacking the trays in the bin, place the fabric across the liquid collection tray at the bottom. The first tray will sit on top of this fabric. Since all the trays are identical, this first tray's bottom is grated like the others to allow for movement of worms. The cloth acts as a barrier to the worms when used at this level, yet it will allow the naturally occurring liquid to pass through for collection below. Depending on the amount of moisture in your bin, the fabric may need to be rinsed when you are ready to harvest compost from your first tray (after about two months). You can easily remove and rinse the silt and castings out of this fabric and reuse it rather than replacing it. Think of it like a reusable coffee filter. It is not unusual to find a couple of stragglers wiggling around down here on the fabric either. Simply place them back in the bedding above.

After applying your liquid-barrier cloth, place one empty tray on top of the cloth and fill it with moist bedding. This bedding will serve as a source of moisture and protection for your worms. It is also a part of their diet; worms actually eat their bedding. Bedding will be added with the addition of each new tray in the future. Through experimentation, you will learn what type of bedding your worms like the most. A commercial bin will likely provide a packaged bedding know as coconut coir to use in your first tray. It is inexpensive and easy to use and may be worth repurchasing in the future. It is always your choice what source of materials to use as bedding and you may prefer to use various recyclable fibers that you already have within your home.

Recommended bedding materials include coconut coir fiber (purchased), shredded newspaper (matte color and black-and-white), cardboard egg cartons, shredded cardboard, interiors of paper towel or toilet paper rolls, and dried leaves. Coconut coir is a very popular bedding choice because of its ease of use. It is very similar to peat moss in its characteristics, yet it is a renewable resource, unlike peat moss. It is a by-product of the Sri Lankan coconut industry and is exported in large amounts in the form of compressed bricks. When rehydrated, this fiber shreds easily and retains moisture. It is a favorite food source for the worms. Though many of the materials used for bedding are a part of our waste stream and therefore free, coir is an inexpensive and convenient source of bedding. Many of my worm clients find it the easiest to use and purchase it regularly when starting new trays. Adding a variety of materials and textures as bedding helps to maximize airflow and moisture retention within the bin. These materials help provide fiber for worms' digestive tracks. In addition, it covers food waste, keeping it, and your home safe from fruit fly infestations.

It is important not to use glossy or photo papers as a source of bedding. These contain chemicals that may harm your worms as well as your compost. It is widely believed now that colored newspaper inks are safe to use as bedding. Most of these colored inks are soy-based and easily digested by the worms. When using safe papers as your main source of bedding, avoid only using newspaper. When moistened, it tends to clump together, limiting airspaces. Adding some cardboard or leaves will make a much healthier living space for your worms and lead to healthy compost.

Some instructions may indicate that the addition of soil is necessary in your bedding preparation. This seems to make sense, right? Worms live within our soil. Yet don't be overly concerned about adding large amounts of soil to your tray preparation. Make sure that you don't actually fill a tray with soil as your starter bedding. Remember, the worms will be making a component of soil as they consume your waste and the surrounding bedding. The transformation is remarkable and should not be missed. The addition of a handful of soil is fine for the first tray to provide some basic microorganisms and familiar particles, but the worms will be bringing along their own working team of microorganisms on

Recommended Bedding Materials

- Coconut coir fiber
- Shredded newspaper
- Cardboard egg cartons
- Shredded cardboard
- Paper towel or toilet paper rolls
- Dried leaves

Coconut coir fiber

their skin and in their gut as well. As they slither and wiggle through the materials in the bin, they will inoculate the tray with these microorganisms who will then take up residence and be a part of the future workings from there on. For the addition of trays, adding a handful of the finished compost on top of new bedding will be helpful to speed up the process.

Moisture is essential in a new tray or bin. Bedding should be moist yet not dripping wet. A basic rule of thumb is that the materials used should have the texture of a well wrung-out sponge. The moisture is important to help with the worms' respiration. Worms breathe through their skin and require the moist bedding to stay healthy. Prepare the bedding source by shredding paper, egg cartons or plain brown cardboard and then moisten it with dechlorinated water if possible (see page 160). If using coconut coir, soak the brick in about 3 quarts (3 liters) of warm water. When it begins to break apart, wring out the excess moisture with your hands and add the coconut fibers to the tray to moisten the newspaper. Add a bit more water, if needed, until all of the paper is damp. The tray should be about two-thirds full of bedding. Adding some dried leaves, sand, and crushed eggshells is beneficial. These substances add grit to the worms' digestive track and act a bit like teeth. Remember, worms don't have teeth but use gizzards to grind their food. The tray is now ready to house worms and eventually their main food source, your food scraps.

New bedding can be added to your first tray after one month to help keep food scraps covered. Also, though bedding retains moisture for healthy worm respiration, add bedding if you notice that the compost is becoming too moist. Shredded paper will easily absorb excess liquid from food waste.

The worms may be a bit dry when they arrive. This moist bedding will rejuvenate them from their travels. After you transfer your worms to this new working tray you can watch them begin to burrow under the bedding.

Starting A New Tray

Harvesting from a migration bin is easy—one of the benefits of using such a system. We will go over these differences later within this chapter. Problems arise when trays and bins are left unharvested for months at a time with compacted contents. Always follow the directions provided with your system and harvest as scheduled, at least every two to three months.

After about two months, the contents of the working tray will have transformed into a fine soil. When you see this fine grade of soil, it is time to start a new tray. Place a new, empty tray on top of the working tray, prepare fresh paper bedding, and start feeding this new tray with fresh food scraps. The worms will then begin their upward migration to the new top tray. The lower working tray can remain in place for a couple of weeks to allow all of the worms to vacate to the top tray before removing it for collection.

When the working tray is ready to be removed, move it on top of the new tray. Remove the bin cover and leave it in a well-lit room for a day or two. During that time, stir the compost a couple times a day with a spoon or your hands. The remaining worms within the compost will migrate down and out of the compost to avoid the light. This will ensure that all of the worms have left the compost before you remove it for harvest. During this time, it is fine to continue to feed the working tray below.

Depending on the type of food you give your worms, you may accumulate more or less liquid in the bottom tray. Use the spigot valve to drain this liquid. You can then dilute the "worm tea" with water to make a great houseplant fertilizer. A 50:50 water-to-worm-tea ratio is recommended.

Photo by Amber Gribben

The rich compost will begin to look like coffee grounds when it is ready for harvest.

MAKE YOUR OWN WORM BIN

Composting with worms doesn't have to be expensive. You don't need any fancy containers or equipment to make this magical process occur. The worms don't mind living in affordable housing. You can easily and cheaply make your own worm bin using a 10-gallon (38 liters) plastic storage bin, which cost between ten and fifteen dollars. Worms like dark places, so choose one that's not made from clear plastic and has a tight-fitting lid. Approximately one square foot of surface area is needed for each pound of kitchen vegetable wastes per week. Because worms reproduce quite rapidly under healthy conditions, many individuals chose to start with 1 pound (.5kg) of worms to save on the initial investment. Though this is sufficient for one individual, if starting a worm bin in a household of two or more, this homemade bin can easily house more worms and be more efficient at processing a larger portion

of the household waste with 2 pounds (1kg) (about two thousand worms) to start. This starter batch of 2 pounds (1kg) of worms will process about 1 pound (.5kg) of food per day.

Worms require bedding that is moist but not soggy. Just like in a migration bin, coconut coir, shredded newspaper and cardboard, dried leaves, and a handful of soil work well for the bedding. If using newspaper, tear it long-ways into 1" (3cm) strips, soak it in water, and then wring out the excess water. Make sure to create a bedding depth of about 8" to 12" (20cm–30cm) in your tote. Remember, deeper is not better, these are surface dwelling worms. The risk of compaction in a DIY bin is much greater given the size and shapes of some of the plastic containers used.

Feed your worms a vegetarian diet; they love fruit and vegetable scraps, breads, grains, cereals, eggshells, paper towels and napkins, dead flowers and plants, coffee grounds and filters and tea bags (remove the staples). They hate dairy, fats, meats, feces, and oil. See page 109 for more feeding instructions.

You can now continue to add kitchen scraps by burying under the bedding. Maintaining the right moisture balance is key to keeping the

DIY Worm Bin

Materials:

- 10-gallon (38 liter) plastic storage container
- drill
- shredded newspaper, soil, leaves, or other bedding
- food scraps
- water

Instructions:

1. Drill ten to twenty holes ¼" (6mm) in size in the lid and around the top of the sides of the bin for air circulation.
2. Place 3" to 4" (8cm–10cm) of moist bedding in the bottom of the bin.
3. Add your kitchen scraps. To reduce fruit flies, wash the skins well to remove any eggs and bury the scraps under the bedding.
4. Add the worms and close the lid.

worms happy and reducing fruit flies. Naturally dry bedding, like shredded newspaper dries out quickly. If the bedding feels drier than a wrung out sponge, you can gently spray it with a plant mister. If you have fruit flies, then the bin is too moist, the food scraps aren't completely covered, or there's not enough bedding in the bin.

KEEPING YOUR WORMS HAPPY AND HEALTHY

Whether using a DIY bin or and upward migration system, the addition of the worms is the start of it all. Once your bin is ready to go, it is time to add your workers. Their transition is usually a smooth one but can be made even better when you keep a few things in mind. Worms are stressed by their travel accommodations. Worms are densely packed within their own slightly dry bedding in a porous bag for travel. Seeking safety and possibly moisture, the thousand or more worms will intertwine themselves into a complex mass within their tight accommodations. This is a common behavior for red wigglers that I have come to call the "worm brain."

Your worms have traveled a far distance, and in cramped quarters. Like people, they may be a bit restless or even slightly anxious. It is important to help them acclimate. Add them to their new home shortly after their arrival to ensure good health. If the bin isn't quite ready, sprinkle a bit of water in their travel bag to rejuvenate and hydrate them while you prepare the bin Worms can be dehydrated when packed in dry bedding or after several days of travel and will recuperate quickly when rehydrated. Remember, a worm breathes through its skin and needs moisture for respiration. It has been stated that worms may lose up to 70 percent of their body weight from dehydration when traveling.

I distinctly remember that first moment when I saw what a pound of worms looked like. As I emptied my bag of red wigglers onto the surface of my prepared worm bedding, the sight of a wriggling mass of red little bodies brought a mixture of excitement, terror and, I sadly admit, disgust. A shiver ran up my spine and a strong feeling of doubt passed through my brain. Was I really going to be able to go through with this? Not only did this doubt pass quickly as I got to know my worms, but, I have successfully been able to maintain a worm bin for more than four years.

Turn on a Night Light for Your Worms

Though this may sound silly, it is important to leave on an overhead light the first night the worms arrive. This may help ease their anxiety and also ensure that they don't attempt to migrate out of the box looking for old friends. Escaped worms are rare and have never happened to my clients, but rumor has it that it has happened to others. When the worms are happy, they have no desire to leave the bin. Even with the lid on, the worms will spy the overhead light through the air holes in the sides and top of the bin and migrate deeper to safety, settling in quickly. By the second night, it is safe to assume they are content and leave them in the dark to go about their business.

If you notice worms exiting the bin in the future, keep a bright light on in the room where you store the bin throughout the day and night. Worms do not like the light and will retreat back into the bedding. In this

instance, they may be trying to tell you something. Survival is their main instinct and they may be feeling threatened. It may be something simple. Take note of shifts in the weather: If it is too hot, or if there is rain in the forecast, the worms will migrate up to the roof to cool down or to protect themselves from drowning in the rain. Remember, the worms think they are still in nature, not in your house! If the tray is full of compost and there are no longer any food scraps or bedding, your worms may move upwards to survive as their castings will eventually become toxic to them.

Feeding Your Worms

Though it is fun to feed the worms, especially in the beginning, only add a handful or two of food the first day. After two or three days, look to see if the worms are beginning to process the food, then begin to add more. It is a very common mistake to overfeed the worms in the beginning. It is best to collect food scraps in a container and then add it to the worm bin every three or four days, making sure that the previous food has been

Making Your Worms Comfortable

To make your worms feel right at home, follow these easy guidelines:

1. Give them a drink of water. Drizzle a teaspoon or two of water directly into the bag upon their arrival.
2. Have their new home ready upon arrival or shortly thereafter. Chances are they have been packed for at least twenty-four hours and will thrive in a new more spacious home.
3. To help the worms acclimate to their new surroundings, leave a light on over the bin for the first night. Worms will burrow down deeper into their new home to avoid the light. Settling down into the depths of the bin makes for happy worms.
4. Give them a snack upon arrival and leave them be for the next two days to settle in. No need to overfeed the worms. Bury some food waste within the bedding the first day and wait two days before feeding again.
5. Don't be a pushy new neighbor or friend. Just like us, the worms need a little peace and quiet while they eat. Checking in on them too frequently will stress them out and interfere with their digestion and consumption.

partially consumed. Add food slowly in the beginning to allow the worms to get acclimated to your household's diet. Remember, you may have purchased only 1 pound (.5kg) of worms. These worms will work hard to process you scraps, and may need time to proliferate before being able to consume more food. Chopping food into small pieces, freezing food and bringing it to room temperature, or adding more worms will increase the amount of food your bin will process. Or just wait a couple months; worms reproduce rapidly!

Visualize the tray in four quadrants and add food to different quadrants each time you feed the worms. This allows the worms to finish what they are working on and move to the new food when they are ready. Like you and I, they don't want to be disrupted in the middle of a meal! This pattern may even allow you to recognize some of their favorite foods and determine how quickly they eat.

When feeding the worms, bury the food scraps under the bedding; this will allow the worms to eat in privacy and darkness. This also keeps the food from turning moldy and rotting. Bad smells are the result of rotting food, not the worms, so always be sure to keep the food covered. Fruit flies may be attracted to the food, but they will not be able to find it if you hide it under the bedding.

HARVESTING YOUR CASTINGS

The bin is full and ready to be harvested when it looks like dark, crumbly soil, which usually happens in two to three months. It can be challenging to separate these wiggly worms from their valuable waste in a DIY bin. Though the contents of the bin have undergone an obvious transformation over the last few months, new food has been continuously added on a daily basis and the worms are roaming throughout the mixture of food and finished castings. The goal is not to throw the baby out with the bath water and start over again. You want to maintain our worm workforce and transfer them to the next batch of fresh work on hand when the time is right. The upward migration bin attempts to deal with this dilemma through its design.

One way to harvest the worm castings from a DIY bin is to encourage the worms to do the sorting. Though worms will reingest their waste

Potting Soil Recipe

Worm castings make a great addition to any potting soil mix. These small particles are the finished product of your worm bin and carry numerous readily available nutrients and microorganisms to be utilized by your young seeds and plants. Here is a mix to try at home:

- ¼ worm castings (adds nutrients, organic matter and structure)
- ¼ sand or soil (adds additional structure and texture to the soil)
- ¼ perlite or vermiculite (adds air spaces and improves water drainage)
- ¼ coconut coir or peat moss (improves moisture retention)

Vary your mixture depending on the resources available in your area or the needs of your plants. Adding up to 25 percent worm castings has been shown to enhance the growth and health of your newly potted plants increasing their ability to resist disease and pest infestations. But remember more is not better! Each component has a role in the mix; a mixture dominant in worm castings will be damaging to the plants.

several times, they do prefer a fresh meal eventually. By adding new bedding and fresh food in a designated area, you can encourage your worms to move out of the old digs and into the new so that you can harvest your black gold product. This is similar to the method used in the migration system yet will occur within the single tub space of the bin. To do this, push everything (including the worms) to one side of bin, clearing a space on the other side. Add a combination of fresh, moist bedding to the clean side, bury new food scraps, and wait for the worms to move on over. It may take a few weeks to a month for the majority of worms to catch the trail and migrate, but don't give up, it will happen in time. Most of the worms will move over to the fresh side, and you can begin to scoop out the compost on the other side. Don't worry, if there are a few worms still in the resulting vermicompost and you are going to use it a garden, but you may want to manually remove the worms if you are using it in potted plants.

There are two main reasons to keep up with a regular harvesting schedule every two to three months. Dense, condensed compost from many months of composting becomes thick and sticky making it more difficult to separate out the worms. More importantly, if a bin is ready for harvesting and left too long, it becomes toxic for the worms, so you want to be careful and keep up with a regular harvest.

Another common method of harvesting compost in a homemade worm bin is referred to as "dump and sort." Because we know what our worms like and dislike, we can always encourage desired behavior. "Dump and sort" relies on the worms preference for darkness. Spread a plastic tarp on the ground outside under the sun or in a brightly lit room and empty the contents. Gently form four to six cone-shaped mounds with the contents of the bin. Leave them in the light for ten to fifteen minutes while you prepare new, moist bedding for the worms. Return and scrape off the first 2 inches of fresh black gold castings. The worms will continue to dive downwards as you scrape layer by layer off of the top of the mound. Place castings into a plastic bag or lidded container for future use. When you reach the bottom of the mound you will have a batch of worms ready to be returned to your freshly prepared bin for composting duty.

If you are harvesting compost during the off-season and need to store it, make sure to keep it in a lidded plastic container or bag to maintain moisture. The nutrient-rich substance is most beneficial when moist. Though it will not become harmful to plants when dried out, it loses its nutrients and living nature as it dries. Moist vermicompost is the best bang for the buck!

CREATURES AND CRITTERS

It is normal to find crawling critters in your worm bin that are obviously not worms. Even when kept inside, your worm bin will eventually house various members of the ecosystem that travel in on our apple peels and lettuce leaves. The majority of these critters are helpful in breaking down your organic food scraps and have little or no interest in leaving the worm bin. Your worm bin may also attract:

- sowbugs
- bacteria
- molds and fungi
- pot worms
- centipedes and millipedes

PROTECTING YOUR WORMS FROM PESTS

Your worm bin is a mini-ecosystem filled with many living creatures. As mentioned, many of the small insects are part of the working team. There are a couple bugs that are a real nuisance and should be controlled at the first sign to prevent an infestation.

The most common and probably the most annoying worm bin pests are fruit flies, especially common in the warmer months. Typically, they enter a bin as eggs on the skin of bananas and oranges. You can eliminate this possibility by freezing, scrubbing, or boiling the items prior to feeding

Dump and Sort

- Pour the bin contents onto a plastic sheet.
- Form the contents into cone-shaped piles.
- Because worms avoid light, they will dive to the bottom of the piles.
- After about ten minutes, scrape 2" (5cm) of material off the top of the piles.
- Repeat the process until the piles are gone.

them to the worms. If you do find yourself with a fruit fly problem, you can make a trap using a sweet-sour liquid like vinegar, wine, soda, or fruit juice. Place a few ounces in a jar or a cup and attach a plastic bag or a piece of study paper to the top with a rubber band and poke a few holes into it with the tip of a knife or pen. Attracted to the sweet-smelling liquid, the flies will enter the jar but won't be able to get out.

You may see mites on the surface of the bedding and just below. They are not harmful to the worms unless their populations increase to the point that they deter the worms from eating. The variety of mites attracted to worm bins feed on dead and decaying matter, not live plants, so they are not harmful to houseplants.

Maggots, also known as soldier fly larvae, may be drawn to your worm bin. The maggot commonly seen in a worm bin is grey-brown and about ½" (13mm) long. It is, by far, the least-liked of worm bin critters! It matures into the soldier fly, a large slow-moving fly that lives around compost and lays its eggs there. This fly does not carry disease and is not a housefly. Though you may have a lot of larvae in the bin, few adult flies hatch because the maggot needs a cooler, dryer place to pupate. The worm bin just isn't that place.

What to do about maggots? Worm composters find that these larvae show up in huge numbers, live a short while, and then disappear. So, be patient. Check to see if you have enough bedding in there. You can reduce the likelihood of having maggots in the bin by mixing in plenty of carbon-rich material every time you feed. The flies are attracted by the smells produced when there's excess nitrogen around.

If you absolutely have to get rid of them, you'll have to empty the bin, rinse off the worms (lay them on some kind of screen), and start your bin over with fresh bedding.

Soldier fly maggots are good decomposers, producing good manure that red worms can further process. So, if you can stand their appearance, consider them short-term guests in the worm bin.

TIME AWAY

Going on vacation? Don't worry; worms can live up to a month with little or no attention in a healthy bin. Just be sure to add extra newspaper and cardboard prior to leaving. Don't feel the need to add excessive amounts of kitchen scraps to cover for your time away. If you add too many new food scraps, you run the risk of developing a mold problem because the worms are not able to consume all the food waste. Paper products are a safe addition. Worms will be able to feed on the paper products over a longer period of time. You may also add some additional food scraps, but remember that too much food may cause an unnecessary odor or pests.

9: Sharing the Wealth

"For me, gardening is a form of prayer. Most people have an awareness of life and death, but few have an awareness of life, death, and life again. Gardeners do though."

—Kaya McLaren

Composting is possible for each of us in some capacity. As we adopt a method and begin to decrease our waste stream, we change our perceptions of garbage and maybe some of our consumption habits. We also accumulate nutrient-rich organic fertilizer, often referred to as black gold, to spread far and wide. It is not a coincidence that this substance is named after one our most valued metals as it is full of value itself. Its uses are varied and range from simple to complex.

We can add our compost to house plants, lawns, and gardens for a boost. We can start seedlings with a perfect mix, including a sprinkling of worm castings. We can feed the root line of our trees. We can turn the black gold into our soil before planting our annual vegetable garden. Or we can study the needs of our sick soils and design composts to cure what ails them. We can even brew up some compost tea as a natural chemical-free fertilizer.

Not all compost is the same. Compost can vary in content, microorganism dominance, and nutrients depending on the composition of waste that was transformed, the age of the compost, and the form of application. For gardeners who are ready to take the next step, loads of comprehensive information is available about amendments and what soil needs in order to be truly healthy. Comprehensive guidelines for building and remediating soil is beyond the scope of this book, however *Teaming With Microbes* by Jeff Lowenfels and Wayne Lewis is an excellent jumping-off point for more information.

FINISHED COMPOST

Varied techniques and methods of composting lead to one general product, rich compost. This product goes through many phases on its way to completion. How will you know when it is finished and ready for use? This is a great question, and there are some general guidelines that we will review here.

Though it may take time, as you are managing and adding to your compost, you will see its transformation right in front of your eyes. It will no longer resemble food and yard waste but will become a dark and crumbly substance, similar to coffee grounds. Remnants of old food may be present but the majority of the contents should be sort of fluffy and easily crushed between your fingers when handled. Because different matter decomposes at different rates, it is often necessary to run your compost through a screening process to separate the partially decomposed materials from the finished product (see the screening compost sidebar on page 153). At times, it is necessary to sort out large, undecomposed pieces of waste, such as beets, potatoes, or corn husks that take significantly longer to reveal the rich compost underneath than all other smaller or softer waste. As its appearance changes, so does its odor. It no longer smells a bit like a mixture of garbage when you remove the lid. It begins to smell sweet and earthy. Rotten or moldy smells indicate a problem, and you may need to give more time and attention to the conditions.

If your compost has reached high temperatures, it will also need time to cool down. Wait until it is a neutral temperature to the touch. If it feels warmer than the surrounding temperatures, leave it a little longer to allow the thermophiles to finish their work. The contents will cool when the workload has diminished. Use temperature as your guide in this instance.

These are some of the essential characteristics of finished compost. It is more important in the springtime to allow your compost to fully decompose before use than in the fall. The partially decomposed compost will compete with the new spring plantings for nitrogen if spread before full decomposition. In the fall, it is fine to work partially decomposed compost into your garden in preparation for the next year's planting. The remaining matter will easily finish decomposing by the time you are ready for planting again. This is true with worm compost as well as traditional outdoor compost. Both can be used in varying degrees of completeness.

It is perfectly fine to store compost until it is needed if you have extra toward the end of the season. Keep it in a covered container to keep it from drying out. It is best to use it within six months of harvesting. During this period, the diverse nutrients and soil life are still available. After this time, the nutrients may begin to leach out, leaving a slightly less fertile substance. But never throw it out! It is essential to return it to the soil at some point no matter when and where that is.

BECOME A SOIL STEWARD

Your first goal when working with compost is to add life to the soil in the form of diverse soil microorganisms. This alone begins to create a stronger and healthier soil food web to support your gardening efforts and the planet's efforts to keep us healthy and well fed. Some areas of your growing will respond quicker than others to the addition of compost. The results will depend on the care you have given your soil in the past and

Screening Compost

After harvesting your compost, it is a good idea to sift or screen it to decrease the particle size and remove unfinished materials. Simply place handfuls of compost over a screening device and rub your hand gently back and forth. As the compost falls through the screen, it is broken into smaller particles. Remove large pieces of scraps and return them to the compost bin.

Screening may take a little extra time but it adds to the value of the finished product. Sifted compost is much lighter and easier to work with. The delicate roots of your seedlings and plants will love the airy texture of this fine compost and will flourish with its capacity to retain water. In addition, screening out larger pieces of undecomposed materials will improve the appearance of the garden beds and ensure that the compost is not competing with the plants for nitrogen. When undecomposed matter is left to finish its transformation, it is using valuable nitrogen resources that the plants could be using to thrive.

It is simple to make your own screening device. All you need is a firm piece of ½" (13mm) metal or plastic mesh or screening and a frame to attach it to. The frame should be sized to fit over a wheelbarrow, storage bin, or a bucket where you plan to keep unused compost. You can build a wooden frame, or you may be able to repurpose an old picture frame or window screen for this use. If you are planning on using a bucket for storing your compost, you may also have an old colander that fits snugly inside a bucket to serve the same purpose as a screen. Repurposing an item can bring another added level of satisfaction to your new behavior as well.

Drier compost sifts easier and may not clog up your screen as quickly during the process. Leave compost out to dry overnight before sifting. Remember to throw all of your undecomposed materials back into the compost to help keep the next batch rolling along.

the amount of damage that was done previously by commercial pesticides and chemical fertilizers. In general, beds of flowering annuals will respond quickly along with lawns. It may take a bit more time for the soil under your edible gardens to reach its maximum health and yield.

A key component to adding compost and building a soil food web is that the more you invest in the creation and use of compost and compost teas now, the less work it will take down the road to maintain a great garden or lawn. In addition, you will be ensuring the health of you, your family, and your pets by eliminating the use of chemical-laden fertilizers. Even without these, your plants and lawn will be better looking and more pest- and disease-resistant over time. It is a win-win situation for all involved. How often does that happen?

The Jar Test:
Is Your Compost Finished?

Fully finished compost will not compete for nutrients with your garden plants. If you want to ensure that all of the compost materials are fully decomposed, try this simple jar test. Remember, the nose knows!

1. Remove a hand shovel of dark compost from your bin and place in a jar.
2. Add water until all the compost is fully saturated.
3. Seal the jar with a tight-fitting lid to create an anaerobic environment.
4. Leave the mixture alone for one week. Do not remove the lid during this period.
5. After one week, open the jar to assess the odor of the contents.

Finished compost will have a rich, earthy smell, even after a full week in an oxygen deprived environment. If your compost has a strong, putrid odor, this is a sign that there are still undecomposed materials present. Allow another four to six weeks to pass before harvesting your finished compost. This additional time will allow these remaining materials to completely decompose.

ECONOMY OF COMPOST

Regular applications of compost will even save you money. In addition to being a free fertilizer, the benefits of your compost in the soil will lead to significant reduction in your watering and, therefore, a smaller water bill. According to the EPA, for every 1 percent that you increase your soil's organic matter, you increase the water absorption capacity by 16,000 gallons (60,566 liters) of plant-available water per acre.[1] This sounds complex but the bottom line is we need less water in our garden or lawn when our soil is regularly fed with compost.

Compost is not always considered a fertilizer per se because it does not only feed the soil, it nurtures it for future efficiency and enhances it. In contrast, most of our farming and lawncare practices strip our soil of its value. Compost does not instantly supply a large boost of fast-acting nutrients, but it does supply a range of essential nutrients over time. The key here to understand is that this happens over time. You are not just using compost to instantly improve growth and yield; you are feeding your soil for future use and life. When striving to feed your soil versus your plants directly, you are looking at the big picture, to a distant goal versus just an immediate change. Your garden and plants will benefit for sure, though not by means of a quick boost of short-lived nutrients. Similarly, you may personally feel temporarily satiated by the boost of sugar and carbohydrates after munching a candy bar, but you will benefit in the long-term from leafy greens and fresh fruit that build the strength of your immune system and help to keep your body in balance.

Amending soil with compost may not create the immediate results of larger plants with instantly higher yields, especially if the soil is significantly nutrient-deprived to begin with. Yet, this is when it is needed most. Compost will, in fact, over time, restore the soil's structure, water retention capacity, nutrient storage capacity, and overall texture that supports future plant growth. Even natural fertilizers do not provide this many benefits. Fertilizers tend to function with short-term benefits and, even when natural, may do the job, but they still don't have the long-term nurturing effects of compost. Besides, only 35 percent of chemical lawn fertilizers ever reach

1. Marc Wise, "Spring into Lawn Care with Organic Treatments," A Fresh Squeeze, www.afresh squeeze.com/chicago/articles/spring-lawn-care-organic-treatments (accessed May 6, 2010).

the grass root anyway. The rest is released into the air or seeps into our drinking water supply.[2] Not only is this type of chemical application a waste of money, but dangerous to all living organisms.

The benefits of compost also go a long way. It is not necessary to create truckloads of new organic compost to reap the benefits. Top dressing and amending or adding to your potting mixes or garden beds is a great use for whatever amount of new compost you create. Remember, the benefits are long-lasting and contribute to the overall health of the soil and all the plant life the compost comes into contact with. The benefits of vermicompost in particular are proven to go even further. You are getting an even bigger bang for your buck when you sprinkle vermicompost or castings around your garden. What does this mean in practical terms? You need less to make a difference. Whether you create a bucketful each year or a truckload, it is enough to start making change.

ENRICHING SOIL AND PLANTS

As you now know, it may take three weeks or two years to harvest your first full batch of compost. There are so many variations in the composting process that it is hard to predict when your first batch will arrive. But once you have successfully harvested a dark and earthy batch of compost, what do you do with it?

Though all plants can benefit from the addition of healthy soil around their roots, each plant has a different preference for nutrients.

 Heavy Feeders: Tomatoes, eggplant, peppers, cabbage, kale, and broccoli. Light Feeders: Turnips, carrots, parsnips, leeks, and onions.

Like some humans, some plants are light feeders and some are heavy feeders. You can choose to prepare a garden patch prior to planting by digging in compost to the upper layers, adding about 2" (5cm) of compost to the surface area of the garden as a good general rule. Many of the most popular garden veggies really appreciate a hearty meal of compost nutrients. Top feed or dig in compost around these veggies throughout the season as well. Heavy feed-

2. Ibid.

ers include: Tomatoes, eggplant, peppers, cabbage, kale, and broccoli. In contrast, some of the root vegetables, such as turnips, carrots, parsnips, leeks, and onions, prefer a lighter meal. Use compost more sparingly around these areas of the garden or add it only at the beginning and end of the growing seasons.

Compost is great for increasing the viability of seedlings as well. Be carefully to use very finely sieved compost with small particles to accommodate the fine root system development. Mix compost with potting soil, perlite and/or sand to start new seedlings indoors early in the season. Do not use compost alone to start the seeds. More is not better in this case. When using worm casting, even less castings are needed to make a significant difference. Adding castings to a potting mix will do the job.

Trees and lawns also thrive from the addition of compost. If you have enough compost to spread around, add 1" or 2" (3cm–5cm) in a ring around the trees. Make sure to spread the compost beyond the drip line or leaf canopy of the tree. This will encourage root growth outwards and help the tree to thrive. The key to a lush and hearty lawn is strong root growth. The addition of compost before sodding or seeding a new lawn will firmly establish root growth. For lawns already in place, sprinkle an application of finely-screened compost directly onto the green blades. As you water or as the rain falls, the compost will work its way deeper, feeding the roots below. Repeat yearly to keep building the immune system of that healthy lawn.

BREWING COMPOST TEA

"Compost tea" refers to the nutrient-rich liquid extract produced when you dissolve finished compost (vermicompost or traditional compost) in room temperature water. Making a batch of compost tea can be another simple and efficient use of our valuable waste stream. Liquid amendments and fertilizers are often easier to apply to gardens and houseplants and can extend the benefits of solid compost much further. Compost tea can be made from a handful of worm castings or a handful of your finished outdoor compost. The resulting tea varies in its nutrient contents depending on the makeup of the compost used and the technique used for brewing, yet it is safe, effective, and inexpensive.

When brewing a cup of your favorite Earl Grey tea, the water darkens as the tea leaves leach their flavor into the boiling water. Making compost tea is similar; you are leaching the valuable resources out of the solid compost to use in a liquid form. In the case of compost tea, room temperature water is sufficient to "steep" your compost. Time may be more important. The nutrient-rich compost releases its nutrients, as well as its living microorganisms, when dissolved over time. This results in a fantastic source of highly concentrated, living, liquid fertilizer and soil amendment. In the liquid form, the benefits of compost can be spread a long way. After steeping for twelve to thirty-six hours, the resulting brown liquid mixture is ready for instant use on the garden and houseplants. Directly drenching the soil and roots around a plant is the most direct way to apply compost tea. Some claim that using compost tea as a foliar spray is also effective; many plants can absorb nutrients directly through their leaves in addition to their roots.

Though compost teas are widely used and valued in agriculture today, there is little research on the specific guidelines for production and application. A general guideline is that a little goes a long way. The days of "more is better" are over when using organic fertilizers. When we bring life and natural balance to the soil, plants do not need massive doses of nitrogen and other nutrients to thrive. They have a supportive environment and a healthy immune system to fight off disease, leaving them free to grow and produce vibrant fruits and blooms. There is no need to spend excessive amounts of time and money reapplying nitrogen-rich chemical fertilizers. Compost teas bring balance and vitality in small doses and infrequent applications. Try watering with tea when transplanting your plants to combat the stress. Then apply some monthly as a boost. For lawn care, one application early in the season as new growth shows and one in the fall when the leaves start falling to the ground is recommended.

Researchers in the Soil Ecology Laboratory at The Ohio State University are specifically studying the effects and use of vermicompost teas (which I like to call worm tea). These studies have demonstrated that worm compost is especially well-suited for brewing compost teas, even better than traditional compost. It is thought that vermicompost has much more microorganism diversity than traditional compost that has been created with high temperatures. These high temperatures are essential for killing off

Compost Tea

1. Dissolve approximately one cup of compost (preferably worm castings) in a 1-gallon (4 liter) pitcher of dechlorinated water. (Using dechlorinated water when preparing your compost tea will prevent the destruction of beneficial bacteria and microbes in the living compost.) If using a 5-gallon (19 liter) bucket, dissolve approximately four to five cups of compost. Stir contents thoroughly and let sit.

2. Allow compost to steep for a minimum of twelve to thirty-six hours. The more time the compost has to dissolve the more nutrients will be released.
3. Stir your tea mixture to increase the rate of nutrient release. Agitation of the mixture breaks down the particles' barriers, releasing nutrients for easier use by your plants. Using an aquarium bubbler will provide ongoing agitation and can be very helpful to speed up this process.
4. Apply your tea with a watering can or spray directly onto leaves with a spray application device. For best results use your tea immediately after steeping.

weed seeds and other pathogens but also kill off much of the biodiversity in the microbial communities. The initial studies surrounding worm tea show significant horticultural benefits including improved plant growth, fruit and flower yield, and possible disease and pest suppression that exceeds that of traditional thermophilic compost tea. This early research has demonstrated the potential for worm teas to possibly suppress difficult-to-manage soil nematodes, plant diseases such as Pythium, and destructive garden pests such as aphids, cucumber beetles, spider mites, and tomato hornworms. Though this substance is proving to have almost magical benefits in our soil and garden, obviously compost tea is for consumption by plants, gardens, and lawns alone, not humans!

DECHLORINATED WATER

Chlorine is a naturally occurring and abundant natural element. It has become one of the most potent weapons against a wide array of life-threatening infections, viruses, and bacteria for over 150 years. Chlorine has made clean drinking water a possibility for many across the globe, protecting us from water-borne diseases. Yet, chlorine is not always helpful in our drinking water. Many, including myself, choose to dechlorinate

> Chlorine has made clean drinking water a possibility for many across the globe, protecting us from water-borne diseases.

drinking water prior to use. It is also a problem to use chlorinated water in aquariums and in compost tea. In these instances, chlorine kills the life forms we are trying to support—our fish and our microorganisms! It is essential to dechlorinate your water before starting a tank of fish as well as before brewing a pitcher of compost tea.

Most municipal water supplies are treated with chlorine, chloramine, or both. They kill off pathogens and harmful bacteria that get into the water or that exist in the pipes as the water is transported between locations. If your water contains only chlorine, it is quite easy to eliminate. Exposing the surface of the water to air in an open container will allow the volatile element to evaporate. Allowing the water to stand open overnight should be a sufficient amount of time to ensure that the chlorine has evaporated. If you aerate the water with a bubbler, it will increase the surface area and increase the process of evaporation.

Unlike chlorine, which evaporates quickly, chloramine takes a bit more effort to remove from your water source. Removing chloramines from your water source requires a reverse osmosis filter, or installation of a simple faucet or under-the-counter, tap-water-drinking, carbon-type filter. Because of its hearty makeup, chloramines can exhaust carbon cartridges much faster than chlorine alone, therefore, filter cartridges need to be replaced more often. Buy a filter that indicates clearly when it is time to change cartridges.

DERAIL THE TOXIC TRAIN

As familiarity with composting and its benefits grows, the use of chemical fertilizers will inevitably decrease. Yet due to the popularity of lawns and the desire for weed-free yards, chemical fertilizers are still big business. In fact, suburban lawns and gardens receive more pesticides than agriculture, up to 3.5 times as much![3] Chemical fertilizers and pesticides are not without a deadly downside. There is no time like the present to derail this toxic train once and for all and embark on a new path with composting and its partner, organic lawn care. Ninety-five percent of the pesticides used on residential lawns are considered possible or probable carcinogens according to the American Cancer Society and the EPA.[4] One out of seven people are negatively impacted by chemical lawn care products.[5] Exposure to pesticides, such as weed killers, are linked to increased rates of miscarriages and the suppression of the nervous, endocrine, and immune systems.[6] Suppressing our natural systems has a similar effect as killing our soil. Our lives are dramatically affected, and health suffers.

Wildlife and pets also suffer. We frequently hear about anomalies and growth defects in amphibians due to chemical runoff. Of thirty commonly used lawn pesticides, sixteen are toxic to birds, twenty-four to fish and aquatic life and eleven are deadly to bees.[7] If exposed to an herbicide-treated lawn, the family dog may also be more susceptible to bladder cancer and twice as likely to develop canine lymphoma.[8] Why would we want to knowingly harm the very pet we are creating a loving bond with or the creatures we can take so much joy in watching and learning from? Is a green lawn really worth it? Isn't there any other way to achieve healthy growth? Of course there is! Organic lawn care methods work to create healthy lawns safe for us and our pets to enjoy.

3. Daniel Pimentel, *CRC Handbook of Pest Management in Agriculture*, 2d ed. (Boca Raton: CRC Press, 1991).

4, 5, & 7. Marc Wise, "Spring into Lawn Care with Organic Treatments," A Fresh Squeeze, www.afresh squeeze.com/chicago/articles/spring-lawn-care-organic-treatments (accessed May 6, 2010).

6. Annie R. Greenlee, Tammy M. Ellis, and Richard L. Berg, "Low-Dose Agrochemicals and Lawn-Care Pesticides Induce Developmental Toxicity in Murine Preimplantation Embryos," *Environmental Health Perspectives* (January 2004).

8. Lawrence T. Glickman, Malathi Raghavan, Deborah W. Knapp, Patty L. Bonney, and Marcia H. Dawson, "Herbicide exposure and the risk of transitional cell carcinoma of the urinary bladder in Scottish Terriers," *Journal of the American Veterinary Medical Association* 224, no. 8 (2004): 1290–1297.

Kitchen Scrap Composting:
For Time-Cramped People

Three common kitchen scraps, usually found in the garbage, can instantly be used to enhance soil even without an official compost pile or worm bin. If it's still too overwhelming or time consuming to start

a full-blown compost effort, try implementing these simple procedures and consider yourself a composter in training:

Egg shells: Egg shells have approximately a 98 percent calcium composition, providing the benefit of added calcium to the soil when deposited there. Soil calcium is necessary for overall plant functioning and health. Without soil calcium, plants tend to lose their color, have a short life, and produce little or no fruit. Simply adding eggshells alone to your soil will increase its health. Resulting plants will have stronger roots and better growth rates than a plant in calcium-deficient soil. Simple ways to use egg shells include: planting seeds directly in dried shells with a bit of soil; crushing shells and turning them into the surface of the soil; or spreading shells on the soil surface around plants and trees. Crushed-up egg shells are also frequently used to reduce the presence of slugs and other small pests known to terrorize tomato plants. Those soft little bodies don't like to drag themselves over sharp shells to get to their meals. It may seem a bit cruel, but your tomatoes will thrive.

Coffee grounds: Coffee grounds are a great source of several nutrients needed in the soil and in plant growth including, nitrogen, calcium, and magnesium. In addition, coffee increases the acidity levels in the soil for plants that prefer an acid-rich environment, such as blueberries, rhododendron, and azaleas. Sprinkle used grounds around plants and water them in, ensuring that they don't dry up on the surface, or till them into the top layer of the soil. To prevent mold if sprinkling your coffee grounds on indoor plants, dry them first or make sure to completely turn them into the soil.

Banana peels: Banana peels are a natural source of the phosphorus and potassium found in expensive fertilizers. So after breakfast, save that banana peel and add it to the dirt to improve the soil fertility. Though peels decompose fairly rapidly, it is a good idea to bury them under the soil so that neighborhood animals don't cart them off. Another great way to use them is to either cut them into small pieces and bury or mulch around the base of trees and plants, or blend them up with some water and pour them right into the soil. Rose bushes in particular benefit from added potassium.

Just because the fertilizers and pesticides are applied outdoors doesn't guarantee that your home is the safe haven that it should be. Residues of weed killers and other lawn chemicals drift or can be tracked indoors where they contaminate the air, surfaces, and carpets and increase children's exposure. Exposure levels inside the home are ten times greater than they are during application.[9] The need to utilize harsh chemical pesticides decreases with a healthy, vital lawn and garden. Compost helps to create this healthy growth.

SIMPLE COMPOSTING

There are many simple methods of minimizing your yard waste and returning nutrients directly to the earth without officially starting a compost bin or heap. I like to call this simple composting. Some methods actually create a useful compost product, such as leaf mold composting. Others, like grasscycling and mulching, compost and transform nutrients right where they land. Simple composting includes some of the most cost-effective methods of minimizing your waste stream because most don't require any special equipment at all. The methods outlined on pages 163–170 may also be great ways to supplement your indoor composting efforts. If you have a worm bin or Bokashi bucket for most of your kitchen scraps you may choose to manage your yard waste by mulching or creating some leaf mold. Remember, there is not just one way to compost. Be creative in your efforts. Mix it up. Try something new. Grasscycling, mulching, and leaf mold composting are simple, inexpensive to start, and still produce healthier soils and reduce your waste stream.

Grasscycling

It has long been a common practice to rake and bag up grass clippings after mowing the lawn. These clippings usually end up in a municipal landfill to remain undecomposed for who knows

9. Ruthann Rudel, David E. Camann, John D. Spengler, Leo R. Korn, and Julia G. Brody, "Phthalates, Alkylphenols, Pesticides, Polybrominated Diphenyl Ethers, and Other Endocrine-Disrupting Compounds in Indoor Air and Dust," *Environmental Science & Technology* 37, no. 2 (2003): 4543–4553.

how long. Over the years, some municipalities have banned yard waste from landfills, encouraging composting. In recent years, some of these bans have been lifted due to the new technology of sequestering energy from the methane gases anaerobically produced in landfills. The jury is still out regarding the efficiency and long-term benefits of creating this type of energy from methane. In the meantime, it seems to make sense to utilize yard waste by grasscycling. This also decrease transportation costs and energy expenditures connected to hauling away yard waste.

Though I am definitely in favor of the physical exercise logged during the raking and bagging of grass clippings, it is a missed opportunity to feed our lawns and the ground underneath. Not only is this one of the easiest ways to start composting, it is free fertilizer for your lawn; grass clippings are a nutrient-rich organic matter. Why waste those valuable nutrients? According to the California Integrated Waste Management Board, lawns generate approximately 300 pounds of grass clippings per 1,000 square feet annually. This can be as much as 6½ tons per acre each year. Much is lost when this ends up in a landfill; the nutrients are unable to return to the soil below and valuable landfill space is wasted on this organic matter.

 It takes around 500 years for nature to produce an inch of topsoil.

Grasscycling is the practice of leaving grass clippings on the lawn when mowing to decompose and return nutrients back into the soil. Like traditional composting methods, grasscycling reduces waste, saves time and money, and restores soil health. Increasing surface area increases the speed of the breakdown of organic materials, so the smaller the grass trimmings, the faster they will breakdown. Also small clippings will help to ensure that the growth of the grass beneath is not inhibited.

To most effectively feed your clippings back to your yard, follow these guidelines:

- Mow the grass when it is dry. Wet grass will clump together instead of spreading over the surface of the grass evenly.
- A mulching lawnmower works great for grasscycling but any mower can be used. If your mower has a collection bag, remove this so the clippings are free to scatter. Check to make sure you

have a safety guard around the opening. If not, you may want to contact the retailer to get a retrofit kit to ensure safety from flying objects.

- Check to see if your mower has a mulch setting. Using a mulching/recycling mower will help to keep the clippings small and will scatter the clippings randomly across the yard and into the soil where they can go to work.
- Follow the "one-third rule:" Mow the lawn often enough so that you're only removing one-third of the length of the grass blade each time.
- If your grass is overgrown, mow it twice. The first mowing should be set to a higher setting to remove about 1" to 2" (3cm–5cm). Once the grass is a bit shorter, change to a lower setting for the second mow. The clippings should be about the same size and will not block light and water from the roots of the growing grass below.
- Cultivate a deep and healthy root system in your lawn by practicing moderate watering techniques. Over-watering not only wastes water but it also encourages fast growth and shallow root systems. Excessive growth leads to more mowing, and shallow root systems are more prone to disease and stress damage
- Keep the mower blades sharp. Dull mower blades may shred the ends of the grass blades leaving them vulnerable to disease entry.

If you subscribe to a lawn care service, ask them to consider grasscycling. Many are willing to do this for no extra cost. It actually may reduce your service charges and certainly benefits the environment as well as your lawn.

When mowing your lawn, consider timing. During the peak growing seasons, a lawn should be mowed about once a week. Although the arrival of fall often marks the end of the best growing season, it is an efficient time to practice grasscycling. Simply let the grass grow a little long just before the leaves drop from the trees above. Once the leaves are down, cut the grass and mulch the leaves at the same time. All this goes in the garden for the winter and, by spring, you will have some nice compost to work in just in time for planting. This is a form of leaf litter composting.

Prefer to collect your grass clippings? Even though grasscycling increases the health of the lawn, some people prefer to remove clippings versus leaving them in place to rot. It may also be necessary to collect clippings if you produce excessive amounts of yard waste or if the season is significantly wet. If this is the case, you can use your clippings in other ways to prevent them from landing in a landfill. The nutrient-rich organic materials are an excellent source of nitrogen (green) and may be just the right thing to heat up a cold compost pile, bin, or tumbler quickly. You should add a ratio of about 1:3 of the total mass of the contents of your compost collection. This great source of energy needs to be combined with carbon-rich materials, such as dried leaves and paper, to encourage your team of thermophilic microorganisms to transform everything into a hot compost.

Mulching

Traditionally, mulching is a protective or decorative garden covering used to inhibit weed growth, protect soil from erosion and extreme temperatures, and help it retain water. Mulch is a protective covering of organic matter placed on the surface of the soil. Its makeup varies based on the outcome desired. The best mulches are porous enough to allow air and water to penetrate into the soil. There are many organic mulches, including wood chips, bone meal, and straw commercially bagged and available for purchase. But why waste money on these products when you could use what you have on hand? Many people may not consider mulching to be a form of composting because it's commercially produced, but it is. It can be as simple as collecting and spreading your dry, fallen leaves or grass clippings and putting them to good use instead of sending them off to a landfill or outside facility for composting.

When you use your own yard debris and waste to reduce weed growth and increase water retention, you encourage natural, simple composting. The waste will eventually breakdown and return its gift to the soil. As this mulch is transforming, it is protecting and sheltering your soil. Once it has fully decomposed, it will mix with the soil below and add to its structure, texture, and water retention capacity in the form of a compost.

You are putting organic matter back into your soil when you spread your mulch throughout the garden. Though its makeup varies, all mulches provide water retention, erosion protection, and insulation for the root systems below in addition to minimizing weed growth. Some mulch may supply specific nutrients to the underlying soil over time as an additional benefit, but this is not the primary purpose in most cases. I have heard the process of mulching of natural leaf litter, grass clippings, and twigs described as "composting in place."

Mulching after mowing is an option for your grass clippings that will minimize your waste stream and maximize your soil heath. Grass clipping are a great source of nitrogen for the soil. Add clippings of any size straight from the bag around trees, shrubs, and flowerbeds. Like commercial mulches, this will minimize moisture loss from the soil and control weeds, as well as provide a natural fertilizer as it is broken down overtime. With a water content of 80 to 85 percent, grass clippings will breakdown rapidly for those areas that need a quick dose of nutrients. Mulching with dry leaves will take quite a bit longer to breakdown and are best used in areas where your primary purpose is soil protection and weed suppression.

Finished compost from you pile or bin can also be applied as mulch around the base of plants and edibles. Of course, the nutrient-rich compost will surely nourish the root systems below in addition to providing the other basic benefits of mulches. Most individuals do not have an endless supply of this valuable substance and may chose to use it more sparingly instead. When using compost as mulch, make sure to use fully finished compost to ensure that critters are not attracted to it. If you see undecomposed matter, or recognizable food scraps, sift it out before mulching or wait another month.

At the end of your growing season, even the vegetable stalks, unripened or rotten crop, and leftover vines can become mulch. Chop up this garden debris and spread it over the top of the garden to prepare for next season. Much of this will be broken down quite quickly while the rest protects the soil underneath until the next growing season.

Tips for Mulching:

- As an alternative to raking leaves, use a lawnmower with a bagging attachment to quickly shred and collect the leaves. Leaves that have been mowed or run through some other type of shredder will decompose faster and are much more likely to remain in place than unshredded leaves.

- Apply a 3" to 6" (8cm–15cm) layer of shredded leaves around the base of trees and shrubs. Use 2" to 3" (5cm–8cm) in flowerbeds.
- In vegetable gardens, place a thick layer of leaves between the rows for the dual benefit of a mulch and a walkway.
- To mulch with grass clippings, spread a thin layer (about 1" [3cm]) over your exposed soil in gardens or around trees.
- Always leave a bit of space around trunks and plant stems when spreading mulch. This will feed the soil but minimize the stress to the plant.

Leaf Mold Composting

When fall rolls around and you have an excess of dry leaves, it is essential that you don't waste their nutrients by sending them to the landfill or burning them in your backyard. As we have discussed, mulching is a great way to utilize this natural leaf litter right on site. Another great simple-composting method is called leaf mold composting. This can be done in a number of different ways depending, once again, on your particular space and time constraints. The resulting product, leaf mold, holds up to five hundred times its weight in water and increases the water-holding capacity of soil. Putting it around (but not touching) garden plants

Be Careful!

Not all grasses and leaves are the same and may not be beneficial when used as mulch. Avoid using walnut, eucalyptus, and camphor laurel leaves. They contain substances that inhibit plant growth. Compost these leaves fully before using them in your garden.

Do not mulch with Bermuda grass due to its highly invasive nature. Many gardeners refer to it as "devil grass" because, before you know it, you may be cultivating Bermuda grass where you meant to be growing strawberries!

will help keep moisture at their roots during summer months, reducing the need for watering.

Leaf composting is also an easy alternative to landfilling leaves. Left to their own accord, the leaves will slowly turn into leaf mold on their own. The entire process occurs naturally over two or three years when left unassisted. Most of us purposely choose not to leave our leaves on the lawn to allow this. Search around a wild forest floor and you will see this very transformation taking place. Layers of leaves will be in various phases of decomposition on their way to creating this rich substance. In your simple composting efforts, you can speed the process up by collecting the leaf litter and encouraging the microorganisms to start their feeding frenzy by collecting, chopping, watering, and tending to them.

Building a large pile of leaves (3' × 6' [1m × 2m]) or collecting leaves in a plastic bag or air permeable builders bag is the way to start. Just like most forms of composting, if the surface area of the contents increases, the process of decomposition is faster. So shred the leaves, run over them with your lawn mower, or crush them within the bags before wetting them for quicker results. Using a lawn mower with a bag is a good way to pick up the leaves because they'll get chopped up and be ready to compost quickly. One disadvantage to this method of simple composting is the quality of finished compost is somewhat inferior to traditional compost. Because leaf mold compost is composed primarily of leaves alone, its diversity in microorganisms and nutrients is limited. Other more labor-intensive forms of composting tend to have a significantly higher level of diversity both from an input and output perspective.

Shrubs, such as azaleas and rhododendron, especially like leaf mold. Though the majority of plants prefer a more nutrient-rich form of compost, these flowering woodland shrubs prefer the highly acidic and low biodiversity of this compost.

In addition to bag composting, stockpile your leaves in autumn if you have a compost tumbler or heap. If you frequently find yourself short on brown material throughout the year, use a little at a time to add carbon-rich materials to your compost. Instead of actively leaf mold composting your leaves, you can place them dried in an empty garbage can and store them to use later.

Instructions for pile composting

- Crush collected fallen leaves.
- Add a shovelful of dirt, manure, or finished compost to activate the microorganisms.
- Pile at least 3' (1m) high and 4' (1.2m) wide as long as you like.
- Water the pile thoroughly to ensure moisture all of the way through to center.
- If you live in a dry climate, thread a soaker hose through the center of the pile and cover it with a plastic tarp to keep moisture consistent.
- To ensure airflow throughout, turn and aerate the pile as contents pack down and become compressed.
- Within two months you will have leaf mold compost ready for use.

Instructions for bag composting

- Collect fallen leaves and place them in bags until two-thirds full.
- Crush the leaves (if you haven't already) by walking on the bag.
- If using plastic bags, poke holes all over to encourage air circulation.
- Thoroughly wet the leaves, making certain that the center is moist.
- Add a shovelful of dirt, compost, or manure to activate the microorganisms at work.
- Shake the bags and tie them closed to keep in moisture.
- Continue to shake the bags every other week and add water; the leaves dry out quickly.
- In two to three months, you'll have rich, dark, leaf mold compost.

Chickens as Compost Assistants

There is increasing interest, even among city folks, in owning chickens. There is nothing like fresh eggs, and knowing where your food is coming from is becoming more important. Having access to these backyard chickens is becoming possible for many, but, owning chickens provides you with more than just fresh eggs, if you know how to recruit them for what they do best. Chickens process all kinds of organic wastes and leave behind nutrient-rich fertilizer. Chickens can be easily employed as your compost main-

tenance crew. Letting chickens roam around your compost pile or heap will make composting more efficient. As the chickens snack on the abundance of organic scraps on your pile, they will naturally turn and aerate the pile, ingest large bugs (that may be less than desirable to see when dumping scrap), and  deposit fresh doses of rich, organic fertilizer as they roam. You and your compost will be happier. There will be less work for you, and the chickens help create just the right texture of compost, which will reap a great product. This is a great example of permaculture in action. By looking at the big picture and allowing nature to guide you, you stay connected to the natural creatures that enhance existence here on Mother Earth.

Chickens will not only help your compost pile, they will also help you to maintain an organic lawn. Chickens are experts at finding bugs, eating weeds, pooping, and scratching (otherwise known as aerating you lawn). Allowing the chickens to randomly wander and deposit their organic fertilizer as they scratch across the surface of your lawn is another great idea. But I have to say the greatest invention since sliced bread may just be the "chicken tractor." When housed in a bottomless, mobile coop, the chickens can be strategically moved throughout your lawn to do their magic in an organized fashion. There are several classic designs to choose from but I encourage creativity when building your own. Add some flare to your chicken tractor!

10: Trouble Shooting

> "Always leave the earth better than you found it."
>
> —Rupert Stephens

As with all first time adventures, there will be some unexpected events and a bit of a learning curve when initiating your composting efforts. Don't expect perfection from the start. Mistakes or roadblocks may occur. This is part of the wonderful human realm we live in. This is how we learn and evolve. You have gathered the initial information and facts; get started, no need to wait any longer. But don't forget to keep your senses alert.

Watching what your compost is telling you will lead to continued success further down the road. Be an astute observer; take in all of the details—the look, the feel, the smell, the color, the critters. The richer your experience of these details, the better. Learn to recognize your cast of characters within the mini-ecosystem called your compost bin or worm bin. In doing this, you will not only nip problems in the bud, but you will be fully engaged in your role as a composter.

COMMON PROBLEMS WITH OUTDOOR COMPOSTING
Yuck! My compost bin smells!

Chances are there is not enough oxygen circulating through your bin and the anaerobic bacteria are having a field day. When oxygen levels decrease, the smell increases dramatically making everyone unhappy. There are three main reasons for this to happen:

1. Compacted contents have minimized room for air to circulate. Aerate the bin by turning the contents or use an aerating tool or a pitchfork to increase airflow deep within. In the long run, you can add piping or tubing in the center of the bin or pile to ensure that the central contents remain oxygenated.

2. Over-watering has caused water to pool and possible mold formation. This type of mold will eventually emit a nasty odor. Turning and aerating the pile or bin should discourage further mold formation as well as begin to dry out the existing materials.

3. There is too much nitrogen from yard and kitchen waste and not enough carbon. An ammonia smell will be a clear indicator that this is the problem. Turning the pile will let in more oxygen and release the ammonia gases. Make sure to add some carbon content, such as straw, twigs, dried leaves, or sawdust, to bring a balance back to the bin.

My compost pile (or bin) is dry.

A dry compost will petrify, not decompose, so it is important to make certain that the contents of your pile or bin are equally moist throughout. Often, the outer layer will appear to be sufficiently moist, but when you go to turn your contents, you will be sad to find large areas of undecomposed dry matter within. To prevent this, moisten layers of materials as you initially add them and make sure that you add the proper mix of brown (dry) and green (wet) materials. Food itself has a high moisture content, especially

those healthy kitchen scraps. For example, lettuce has 87 percent water content versus newspaper, which only has about 5 percent. Adding moisture may simply be adding the right mix of scraps. It may also be necessary to aerate your pile for the purpose of water percolation as well as oxygen flow itself. Create some spaces within the contents for water to flow easily.

Watering the compost is necessary at the very start as well as further along the way. Rainwater is a great, inexpensive friend. You can increase the capture of rain in an open heap by creating a bit of a saucer shape in the center to capture the water so that it doesn't run off the top.

Get in the habit of checking the compost daily if possible, especially in dry climates. As you water your bin or the materials you are adding, make sure to use a gentle spray to thoroughly dampen the dry areas and materials. Your goal is not to flush out your materials with a hard blast of water; many of the nutrients will be lost as excess water leaches out the bottom.

There are lots of bugs in my bin.
Most bugs are a good sign that you have a healthy compost pile. Don't be overly concerned that these creatures are interfering with the process of decomposition. The presence of some critters, such as maggots, is just plain undesirable to some people and you may want to limit them. Maggots are the offspring of the common housefly. These and other types of flies tend to really love a good compost pile, especially the insulating layers of moist straw on top. When the parents can make their way to the surface layers and lay their eggs, there is little to do to deter them from hatching.

Once again, prevention is the key. Covering your open bin or pile with a layer of screening, loose soil, or a piece of sod will deter the parents and minimize maggots.

My pets are attracted to my compost bin.

Be careful about what you are adding to your bin. If you are adding meat or dairy, you can't blame your pets for being interested. A well-balanced compost bin will not smell like roses, but should not be attracting too many hungry animals. If they are still interested, just make sure you keep a heavy rock or brick on the lid (if your bin is covered). If you have an open heap you may need to contain it if you have curious pets.

My compost doesn't seem to be doing anything!

Unless your compost is extremely dry and beginning to petrify, it is decomposing. The rate at which compost decomposes varies dramatically based on its contents, maintenance levels, and its surrounding temperatures. It can take more than a year for the full transformation to occur when the mid-temperature bacteria are the primary workers. If you would like to try to speed up your compost, try to kick-start the high-temperature thermopiles with some high-nitrogen materials. Dried horse, cow, chicken, or rabbit manures work quickly (see the sidebar about manure on page 79). Simple store-bought options to heat up a pile also include dried dog food and rabbit feed that contains plant and protein meal. Another option that doubles in the garden as a pesticide and fertilizer is blood meal. Some have expressed apprehension about using animal blood in their compost, yet it is widely viewed as an effective option as an activator. There are commercial activators on the market as well, but reviews seem to be mixed. The best thing to do is to get the hot workers on your team by adding the right mix of ingredients as you go. Once the team is on board, Mother Nature tends to take over.

There are hard, dried pieces of food in my bin.

It is important to keep all of the materials within your bin equally moistened. This includes the center of your pile as well as the edges. Portions of your compost will naturally dry out faster than others and will need a dose of water to kick-start the decomposition again. In addition to this, some foods will decompose faster than others. It is best to shred or cut rough, woody materials into smaller pieces to hasten their process of breakdown. The more surface area exposed to the hungry microorganisms, the better. When harvesting your compost, just add larger pieces back into the bin and moisten them, they will likely become black gold by your next harvest.

Animals are digging up my trenched compost.

It is essential to bury the food or yard waste at least 12" to 14" (30cm–36cm) deep prevent animals from becoming interested. This is especially true if you are not fermenting the waste with Bokashi enzymes prior to burying. The odor of naturally decomposing waste may attract neighborhood pets or wild animals if it is close to the surface. Avoid trenching meat and dairy wastes to avoid creating attractive odors for neighborhood animals.

My compost pile is steaming.

Temperatures within a compost pile can rise high enough to boil an egg. This will cause steam at times. A hot compost is a sign of thermophiles in action. A transformation is underway. No real need to worry. Continue to turn and aerate the pile as usual. The hot temperatures should cool down within two to three days. A hot compost may heat back up two to three more times as the contents transform.

I harvested my compost, but there were undecomposed items in it.

It is normal for various items in the compost to decompose at various rates. When harvesting compost, separate out the finished matter from the processing matter. You can do this by hand or by using a screening process. Return the undecomposed materials to the bin to continue processing. As new materials are added, microorganisms will combine with the new items and continue to eat, creating a transformation.

A three-bin system works great for this very concern. Each bin will be in various degrees of transformation, new material in one bin, processing materials in the second, and finished compost in the last bin. Materials can be moved through as needed with a clearly defined area for each phase of materials. If you are using a bin or barrel system, simply dump all of the contents, move the bin to a new location, and refill with unfinished and new materials. The finished product can be removed in a bucket or wheelbarrow for use in the garden.

If you use unfinished compost in your garden, you may cause your compost to compete with your garden plants.

My compost is soggy and wet.

If your compost is soggy and wet, chances are it has a bit of a putrid odor indicating that an anaerobic process is starting to take over. This means that oxygen is running out and the community of microorganisms you are trying to support is dying. Remove the lid or covering of your compost. Turn the contents of your compost, tumble, or use an aerating tool to bring oxygen back to the center and surrounding materials. Add some carbon-based materials to soak up extra moisture. The proper feel of a healthy compost is like a wrung-out sponge. Be cautious about adding too many wet kitchen scraps without an accompanying carbon source.

I used compost in my garden and seeds that I didn't plant are sprouting.

Unless your compost has reached high temperatures, the weed seeds and vegetable seeds will not be killed. If they make their way into your garden through your compost, they may germinate with these fertile conditions. To prevent this, make sure that all weeds that you add to your compost have not yet gone to seed or that your pile reaches its high-temperature phase (at least 140° F [60° C]). Remember, the thermophilic bacteria and fungi are sufficient to kill off the weed seeds and ensure that they don't make their way into your garden. Seeds may also have made their way into your compost through manure additives. The digestive track of many animals is not sufficient to kill off seeds.

COMMON PROBLEMS WITH SIMPLE COMPOSTING
My lawn quit growing after grasscycling.

It is important to properly adjust the blades on your lawn mower before grasscycling. If the grass clippings are too large, they may block the light

Helpful Hints:
Outdoor Composting

- If concerned about the appearance of an outdoor compost bin or pile, introduce a trellis around the edge. Plant a heavy-feeder plant that will benefit from the nutrient-rich soil surrounding a compost, such as Primrose. Not only will this beautify your compost pile, it will deter pests.
- Plant nutrient-loving edibles around the perimeter of your compost. This will also maximize the leaching of nutrients and the rich soil organisms that accompany a compost receptacle that has flow-through characteristics (which is not a benefit with a raised tumbler or an enclosed barrel, bin, or cone). The fruiting plants will enhance the visual appearance of a compost and encourage more frequent trips to check its status. More frequent visits means more information about the status of your compost and more opportunities to keep it healthy.

- Keep a bucket or can of soil next to your compost pile or bin and add a handful when you add scraps to help evenly distribute soil microorganisms. Remember, these are strong team members and will help to transform the new waste more effectively when equally distributed.
- Do not add only kitchen scraps to your compost. Kitchen scraps (green) alone can make compost too moist. They have a moisture content of approximately 85 percent and the ideal moisture content of a compost pile falls around 65 percent. This means that you need to add dry (brown) materials, such as dried leaves, straw, untreated sawdust, newspaper, and cardboard to keep the pile healthy.
- When collecting kitchen scraps in a small countertop collector, line it with a biodegradable bag or newspaper to increase the ease of cleaning your receptacle and transferring your waste to the outdoor compost. Remember, both biodegradable bags and newspapers can be thrown directly into a compost and will become black gold in short time.

from your existing grass. It is sometimes necessary to mow twice if your lawn is overgrown. The proper length of your clippings should be approximately 2" (5cm) in length.

It seems like I have more worms and bugs in my soil since I mulched.
Great news! Your ecosystem is expanding! This is an added benefit from mulching, not a problem. Worms are attracted to the new layer of organic matter on the surface and begin to move in and consume it. Worms attract more worms and worm castings attract all kinds of soil food web creatures. Your mulch is increasing the diversity in your soil. You are growing an entire sustainable ecosystem.

After mulching around my tomato plants, the stems seemed to rot a bit.
Though mulches can help a plant to thrive by assisting with water retention and weed suppression, it is important not to apply mulch directly around the base of the stem. The microbial activity alive in a mulch can actually cause some decay on the stems when making direct contact. Keep mulch separate from the base of all trunks and stems. Let it help the surrounding soil food web and then, in turn, help the plant itself.

COMMON PROBLEMS WITH INDOOR COMPOSTING
Yuck! My NatureMill compost bin smells!
Aerobic decomposition does have a smell, but a NatureMill is designed to minimize this for indoor use. Consumers who are using this product recommend adding additional sawdust pellets and baking soda to control or eliminate unusual amounts of odor.

Mold is growing in my Bokashi bucket.
Bokashi is a form of fermentation and should not encourage mold growth. You probably need to add more Bokashi effective microorganisms (EM) mixture on top of newly added food to eliminate this. If the mold is whitish and fine, like spider webs, it is likely a form of fungal growth. It is safe to continue with your bucket, taking extra care to cover scraps in the future. If the moldy growth that you see is green, it is recommended that you dump the contents of your bucket into an outdoor compost or into the

garbage and start again in the manner outlined above. In your future efforts, make sure to sufficiently cover all food scraps with Bokashi EM mix.

I have a lot of liquid in my Bokashi bucket.

Liquid is a natural product of Bokashi composting. It is essential to have a mechanism to drain off this liquid by-product of the fermentation process. Commercial Bokashi buckets have a specific design, including a tray insert that separates liquid from fermenting solid waste and a spigot to make draining easy. If you are using a DIY bucket, make sure to create drainage for successful fermentation.

COMMON PROBLEMS IN A WORM BIN
Yuck! My worm bin smells!

A worm bin is a mini-ecosystem and it is possible for it to get out of balance. When out of balance, it may begin to smell. The most common problem associated with a smelly worm bin is overfeeding. When you continue to add food at a rate that is difficult for the worms to keep up with, the food will inevitably begin to breakdown and decompose. When this happens, it smells! Remember, the worms are actually eating your garbage; you are not encouraging decomposition in this form of composting. If you suspect that food is beginning to decompose, add some new paper bedding over the top and stop feeding for one to two weeks to let the worms catch up.

If the odor continues to be a real problem, remove any large chunks of food and then stop feeding for one to two weeks. You can store your leftover waste in the freezer to reintroduce later when thawed. After freezing, food is much easier for worms to digest and they can catch up quickly. If you are not planning on increasing your worm population by adding another pound (.5kg) of worms to handle the load, try pureeing your scraps before adding them to the bin. The smaller the waste, the easier it is for the worms to keep up with the load. Remember, worms have no teeth and very small mouths.

If the smell becomes a reoccurring problem, you may want to supplement with another form of composting, such as a Bokashi bucket, or add another pound (.5kg) of working worms. You likely have a lot of waste and you need to be realistic about your composting requirements.

The worm castings are wet, heavy, dense, and difficult to remove.

How long has it been since you harvested your worm bin castings? Usually castings become very dense and hard-packed when left in a bin for a prolonged period of time. Not only does this make it difficult for you to harvest your product, it is not a healthy environment for your worms. Though worms will reingest their waste several times making a very pure grade of castings, eventually a buildup of dense excrement gives off gases and becomes toxic for the worm population. The best method, as in many cases, is prevention; harvest your bin at least every two to three months. If the castings are already too dense, it may be a bit late to harvest, so it is important to try to aerate the contents of the bin to add oxygen as well as decrease the moisture levels. Remove the lid in a well-lit area (remember, worms don't like the light and will not be tempted to hit the road for healthier homes if the light is on). Stir the contents of your bin to introduce air to the lower levels. Leave the lid off for a day or so until the contents dry a bit. Begin to harvest your castings and reintroduce new fresh bedding and food scraps. Another recommendation is to encourage some symbiotic plant growth to naturally aerate the castings. By germinating some fast growing seeds, such as bird seed, along the surface of your bin, you are encouraging the roots to reach down to aerate the lower levels. In addition the sprouting, plants utilize the carbon dioxide given off by the waste and the worms will utilize the added oxygen given off by the plants. My worm bin usually has some sprouting peppers or cucumbers from my leftovers. Eventually, you will turn over and bury the plants, which will become food for the worms.

My worms are crawling up the sides and trying to escape!

Worms will migrate throughout the bin looking to cool down, if they sense a storm on the horizon, or to socialize in new areas, but mass migration is different. When worms become unhappy, they will look for a new home. In a balanced worm bin, this is very rare. Conditions that may lead to a mass migration up and out like this are an extremely wet bin, a dry bin, or a very acidic bin. Adding new bedding in the form of shredded newspaper, cardboard, egg cartons, or dried leaves may give the worms a shelter from the conditions as you balance out the bin. New bedding will

Faster-Eating Worms

Because worms have very small mouths and no teeth, you may need to assist them with their human-size meals. There are several ways to make their job a bit easier:

1. Puree your food scraps in a blender or food processor before burying them in a bin. Don't worry, worms don't mind mixing carrots and coffee grounds. Make sure to spread out this puree in a thin layer, no thicker than an inch (3cm), and cover with sufficient bedding. Temperatures can rise quickly if the food starts to decompose before the worms get a chance to chow. Though it may not look so appetizing to us, this puree of garbage will be easily and quickly consumed.

Photo by Amber Gribben

2. Freeze your food scraps prior to burying them in the worm bin. This is an especially good option in the warmth of the summer. The added cold food will cool off the bin as well as help to breakdown the food for easier consumption by the worms.

3. Add another pound (.5kg) of worms. The more mouths to feed, the better the rate of consumption. Oftentimes, a household has too much waste for its present worm population. Add another pound of worms and increase the efficiency of your entire bin.

also absorb excessive moisture if this is the problem. Moisten new bedding if dryness seems to be the cause. It may be difficult for you to know if acidic conditions have taken over your bin, but if you suspect this to be the case, crush a handful or two of dried egg shells or powdered limestone and add them to the bin. It is helpful to do this on a regular basis to prevent overly acidic conditions from occurring.

Fruit flies have taken up shop in my bin.

Fruit flies may indeed be one of the most annoying problems to have in a worm bin. We all have had experiences with summertime fruit fly invasions. These little pests enter our homes as eggs on the surface of our fruits and vegetables and proliferate quickly on any exposed food surfaces they can find.

Once the fruit flies have entered, it is essential to take the upper hand and eradicate them as soon as possible. Stop feeding the worms (and the flies) new scraps for one to two weeks as soon as fruit flies become an issue. Use the wand attachment on your vacuum to suck up the flies. Set up your vacuum next to the bin, turn on the vacuum and with your wand in one hand use your other hand to remove the lid of the bin. Immediately vacuum the air in the bin; move quickly to capture the flying adults.

Then create a small trap within the bin using a paper funnel and a small jar or dish (about the size of a bud vase or baby food jar). Fill the dish with apple cider vinegar, balsamic vinegar or beer. Add the funnel to the dish and place it inside the bin to lure the flies. As they descend down into the funnel to taste the sweet-smelling liquid, they will be trapped and unable to leave. Remove the dish and empty its contents after twenty-four hours. Repeat as necessary until all the eggs have hatched and no more adults have entered.

Occasionally, it is necessary to start over with new bedding to completely eliminate an infestation that has gotten out of hand.

Prevention is key! Always wash your fruit and vegetable peels well to remove any eggs that may be on them. Always bury your food in your worm bin. Fruit flies love exposed food scraps. They just can't resist laying their eggs on this source of nourishment. This is their instinct to ensure their young hatchlings survival. Take an extra minute or two to shift some bedding aside and bury the new food scraps at least 1" (3cm) deep within the bin. Keep a small utensil near the bin to make it easy to bury the scraps. Another preventative option is to keep a moist sheet of newspaper on top of your bedding at all times. I have also cut a piece of cardboard to the size of my bin and moistened it for use as an added fruit fly barrier. The worms don't mind. They eventually eat the cardboard and burrow within the ridges along the way.

Mold is growing on the food in my worm bin, is this a problem?

Mold is a natural part of the decomposition process. Having said that, you will keep mold to a minimum by properly burying the food scraps 1"–2" (3cm–5cm) deep in the paper bedding. This will allow the worms to eat the food quickly and will also prevent pests. This is especially important if you know that you have mold sensitivities or allergies.

The worms aren't eating; are they sick?

The worms will let you know when something is wrong. Noticing their behavior is a key to a happy and healthy worm bin. If your worm bin is new and you notice that the worms are not eating, don't worry! The worms often take their time settling into their new surroundings and getting used to your diet and feeding schedule. Give them time and keep watching. If you have an established bin and you notice that the worms have stopped eating, let them catch up. Stop feeding them for two to three weeks. Then check to make sure that they are making their way through the food that has accumulated. Resume feeding them when you see that the food has been composted. You may be overfeeding the worms. Though they work at breakneck speed for their size, they have no teeth and very small mouths. You may need to cut the scraps smaller to help speed up the process.

The worms seem to be hot and sluggish.

On a hot and humid day, I tend to get a bit sluggish myself. Similarly, if the heat rises outdoors or in your worm bins to about 80° F or 85° F (27° C–29° C), the worms will be sluggish and they will not feel like eating much. If the temperatures reach 95° F (35° C) they will begin to die. Move your bin to a shady spot out of direct sunlight. Place some recently frozen food scraps within the bin to cool the inside temperatures. As the food defrosts, moisture will be released and the worms will be able to easily break down the food in this softened form. Monitor moisture levels to make certain that conditions don't become too moist in turn. Another solution may be to place a moist fabric on top of the bin with a fan or breeze directed across it. Like wearing a wet T-shirt, this will help to keep the bin cooler as the moisture evaporates.

My worms are cold and look sluggish.

Similar to a hot worm bin, a cold worm bin will also become dangerous for the worms. They will become sluggish and their appetite will begin to disappear at temperatures around 50° F (10° C). The worms will die near or below freezing. Move your worm bin inside during winter months. If you need to keep your bin in an unheated garage or basement, add some insulation around the bin. Bales of hay, repurposed bubble wrap, and Styrofoam all make great insulators.

I've been eating out a lot lately and don't have anything to add to the bin.

Don't worry, worms reingest their own waste several times before becoming hungry for something new. What may look like brown compost to us may still be a healthy meal full of unprocessed organic food waste for the worms. Finished castings will resemble coffee grounds—fine, granular, dark particles. If it has been a long time since you added scraps to the bin, the bin may be in need of harvesting. If the contents of your bin are looking like rich coffee grounds, then the worms may be in danger and need new bedding and food. An environment of pure castings eventually becomes toxic for the worms. Remember that paper products, such as cardboard, newspaper, and coffee filters are sources of food for the worms as well your food waste. The inside of your toilet paper roll can become a hearty worm meal when moistened and torn up into several pieces.

My worms aren't reproducing like I think they should be.

Research shows that worms can indeed double in number in three months when conditions are favorable. The important thing to consider here is that they do this when *conditions are favorable*. Many different elements contribute to the proper balance of a worm bin, including temperature, moisture levels, populations, and food source. If some of the conditions are less favorable to the worms for reproduction, you may see fewer cocoons in the bin. The best way to ensure normal reproduction is to keep an eye on the conditions in the bin. Harvest the bin regularly to remove castings and keep a steady temperature and food supply. It has been my experience that there is a specific cycle of reproduction in my worm bin, a fertile seasonality of some sort. There seem to be times where the worms are tangled up day and night and other times when they are quiet and still. I am convinced they are very sensitive creatures and there may be many secrets we have yet to uncover about their specific behavior.

I think I have too many worms in my bin.
Too many worms is rarely a problem. The more worms in your bin, the more efficiently they will consume more garbage. Worms tend to regulate their reproduction when circumstances for survival are in question. Over-population would be a reason for self-regulation. Cocoons can lay dormant for several years before hatching if the conditions are not favorable. If you think you have extra worms, share them with a friend.

There are tiny bugs all over the insides of my bin. Will they kill the worms?
There is an entire ecosystem within your bin. The balance of this system can tip at times. When conditions are right for certain critters, they will thrive. The majority of worm bins will contain some small reddish, white, or brown mites. Mites will thrive and proliferate quickly in a very moist worm bin. In general, they are not harmful to the worms and are part of the natural ecosystem, yet if the numbers increase to the point that they completely cover the food, the worms may not continue to feed. They will take a backseat to these small critters. At this point, it is important to restore a balance. To do this, open the bin to reduce the moisture (leave a light on during the evenings). Remove any food or bedding that is covered in mites, wash it off and return it. Lure large numbers of mites to a piece of bread or cantaloupe and remove, wash, and replace as needed to decrease numbers.

Will the tiny bugs that live in my worm bin cause damage to my plants when I transfer the casting over?
No, the small organisms that thrive in a worm bin consume dead and decaying materials. The live plant matter in your houseplants will not be of interest to them. There are methods to kill off potentially harmful organisms in compost through heating processes, such as solar exposure, yet this will also kill off the life in the soil. This life is the benefit of using worm castings in your plants!

The Future Starts Today

"Change is inevitable. Growth is intentional."

–Glenda Cloud

In truth, the future started long before today. The effects of our past choices, as a culture and as individuals, have affected our lives today as well as the lives of future generations. Excess chemicals applied long ago now lie within the depth of our soils, finding their way into our bodies and the bodies of our children. Starving, and often contaminated, soils are producing nutrient-deprived foods for our dinner tables. Newspapers and plastic bags long ago discarded by our parents are preserved in enormous landfills with no future purpose but to take up space. Even the atmosphere surrounding the earth is scattered with tens of thousands of pieces of debris, relics of our past space travels. These unfortunate symbols of industrialization and so called "progress" are evidence of past choices and in some cases poor decisions. Each day, we each have many decisions to make. Intentional choices to minimize our waste and revitalize our soils are within reach for each of us as demonstrated in the previous chapters.

Bringing awareness to the forefront is essential for growth and change. Neither avoidance nor passivity will do any longer. We must, as a society, take it upon ourselves to see our individual responsibility and make individual (and, therefore, eventual societal) changes. These societal shifts have the potential to become global shifts, benefiting the community of Earth as a whole and all the creatures residing together here. As the population on the planet continues to grow, our demands on Mother Earth also grow. As more and more cultures around the globe take on Western lifestyles, we incur more damage through the demands of consumerism and these disposable lifestyles. There is no better time to reconsider your personal lifestyle.

We must not become overwhelmed by the past or the current message that is being revealed to us by our threatened environment. Our energies should be directed in life-giving ways. We cannot change the past nor can we change the behavior of those around us. Yet the actions of each person can and will make a difference in the future. Be an example of change and growth for those around you.

It is only within the present moment that we can act. Each moment, though fleeting, has infinite potential. The immensity of this cannot easily be grasped by our thinking minds, so well-trained for multitasking, maximizing productivity and problem solving, and so often lacking hope and future vision. The choice to become a steward of the environment, whether for the sake of our soils or for the goal of decreasing your waste stream, is necessary. Reuse, reduce, recycle! Composting does all three of these at once. As Susan Strasser so eloquently stated in *Waste and Want*, "Recycling and reuse … remind us of the threads that bind our individual households to the planet and the activities of our daily lives to the future."

Photo by Stephanie Davies

Today is where we can make a difference for the future. Conscious decisions and actions we take in this present moment will determine the health of our planet. Tread lightly on the ground beneath your feet and be careful—not guarded or fearful, but "full of care" for the decisions you make each day.

Resources

BOOKS

Gaia's Garden: A Guide to Home-Scale Permaculture (second edition) by Toby Hemenway, Chelsea Green Publishing, 2001

Worms Eat My Garbage: How to Set Up and Maintain a Worm Composting System (second edition) by Mary Appelhof, Flower Press, 1997

The Earth Moved: On the Remarkable Achievements of Earthworms by Amy Stewart, Algonquin Books, 2005

Teaming with Microbes: The Organic Gardener's Guide to the Soil Food Web (revised edition) by Jeff Lowenfels and Wayne Lewis, Timber Press, 2010

The Complete Compost Gardening Guide by Barbara Pleasant and Deborah L. Martin, Storey Publishing, 2008

The Rodale Book of Composting: Easy Methods for Every Gardener edited by Grace Gershuny and Deborah L. Martin, Rodale Books 1992

Let It Rot!: The Gardener's Guide to Composting (third edition) by Stu Campbell, Storey Publishing, 1998

Silent Spring by Rachel Carson, Mariner Books, 2002

Waste and Want: A Social History of Trash by Susan Strasser, Henry Holt and Co., 1999

Blessed Unrest by Paul Hawken, Viking 2007

In Defense of Food: An Eater's Manifesto by Michael Pollan, Penguin, 2008

MAGAZINES

BioCycle: Advancing Composting, Organics, Recycling, & Renewable Energy, www.biocycle.net

MOVIES

Trashed
Dirt! The Movie
Food, Inc.

INTERNET RESOURCES

www.EarthWormDigest.org, Vermiculture forum and resource site.

 www.urbanwormgirl.com Provides vermicomposting education, worm bins, red wiggler worms, bedding, and "know how."

Index

Books of interest

Keeping Chickens

Chickens can be the perfect addition to your garden. They consume weeds and can provide you with a natural food source. This book shows you exactly how to care for a small flock by covering everything from choosing the right breed to feeding and housing. Plus you'll find fun egg recipes, feather-and-egg craft projects, and even a look at how chickens interact with children and other pets. ISBN-13: 978-0-7153-3625-0; ISBN-10: 0-7153-3625-8, paperback, 176 pages, #Z7135

Living Large on Less

You don't have to be a financial whiz (or even mathematically inclined) to manage your money. *Living Large on Less* is full of hundreds of ways to save money without drastically altering your lifestyle. You can eat the food you want, wear your favorite designer's clothes, take a dream vacation, and throw a great party without breaking the bank. With this advice, you'll never pay full-price again. ISBN-13: 978-1-4403-0432-3; ISBN-10: 1-4403-0432-7, paperback, 224 pages, #Z7133

Organized Simplicity

Simplicity isn't about what you give up. It's about what you gain. When you remove the things that don't matter to you, you are free to focus on only the things that are meaningful to you. Imagine your home, your time, your finances, and your belongings all filling you with positive energy and helping you achieve your dreams. It can happen, and *Organized Simplicity* can show you how. ISBN-13: 978-1-4403-0263-3; ISBN-10: 1-4403-0263-4, hardcover with concealed spiral, 256 pages, #Z6515

These books and other fine Betterway Home titles are available at your local bookstore and from online suppliers. Visit our website at www.betterwaybooks.com.